Praise for *Learning Serverless*

"In this book, Jason covers every important aspect of serverless architecture. Simply put, if you're working on or planning to work on serverless—this is the book for you!"

—*Erez Berkner, CEO at Lumigo*

"Serverless adoption is growing significantly. Jason Katzer's book offers an important overview of what developers need to learn, and what challenges they'll have to overcome, to become productive with serverless."

—*Vadym Kazulkin, Head of Technology Strategy at ip.labs*

"Capital One leverages serverless architecture throughout our organization. Knowing when, when not, and how to manage serverless at scale is a must-have tool for any technology leader in the modern world."

—*Jason Valentino, Senior Director and Head of Engineering, Capital One Shopping*

Learning Serverless
Design, Develop, and Deploy with Confidence

Jason Katzer

Beijing · Boston · Farnham · Sebastopol · Tokyo

Learning Serverless

by Jason Katzer

Published by O'Reilly Media, Inc., 1005 Gravenstein Highway North, Sebastopol, CA 95472.

O'Reilly books may be purchased for educational, business, or sales promotional use. Online editions are also available for most titles (*http://oreilly.com*). For more information, contact our corporate/institutional sales department: 800-998-9938 or *corporate@oreilly.com*.

Acquisitions Editor: Jennifer Pollock	**Proofreader:** Piper Editorial, LLC
Development Editor: Sarah Grey	**Indexer:** nSight, Inc.
Tech Editor: Right Touch Editing	**Interior Designer:** David Futato
Production Editor: Deborah Baker	**Cover Designer:** Karen Montgomery
Copyeditor: Sonia Saruba	**Illustrator:** Kate Dullea

November 2020:   First Edition

Revision History for the First Edition

2020-10-28:   First Edition

See *http://oreilly.com/catalog/errata.csp?isbn=9781492057017* for release details.

978-1-492-05701-7

[LSI]

Table of Contents

Part III. Concepts

This book is dedicated to my loving parents.

Preface

This book will not make you an expert, but it will be an important step of your journey—it will put you in the top half of developers.

The purpose of this book is to help you understand what's important, and what you need to learn and improve on in order to level up in your career or ship your next big personal project.

About This Book

This book is about arming you with the knowledge you need to represent serverless as an important new technology. There are plenty of doubters out there. And there are plenty of zealots. This book is not from any of those, or for any of those. This book is for people who want to write serious software and gain the respect of peers and colleagues by doing it predictably. I didn't choose to defend serverless. I just chose to ship great software in a way that minimizes maintenance as much as possible.

This book will not tell you how to make your use case serverless. Nor should it. This book will tell you how serverless can help you ship amazing software while saving a bunch of time. It will be real and honest with you about where the serverless world stands. If, on the other hand, you already know everything, it will (I hope) reinforce your worldview in a way that you can share with people who "don't get it."

The goal of this book is to serve as a guide for building maintainable and scalable services through the lens of serverless computing. First, we'll align ourselves on what it means to build a production system. Then, we'll discuss knowledge specific to the current world of serverless compute, and the way that you or your team have decided to run your serverless workloads.

The underlying ideas and philosophies in the first part of the book are meant to be as timeless as a technical tome can be: plan your software for all edge cases and the real world. Use creative thinking and prioritization to spend the appropriate amount of time solving issues that are less likely to occur.

I have been fortunate enough to spend time teaching programming. I have taught students of all ages, and even ones who were learning English at the same time as learning programming. Hopefully, these lessons will be shaped by that experience so a 12-year-old would be able to pick up this book and build something amazing. The same goes for someone who is 88. So bear with me as I talk about some concepts in this book that you may already be familiar with. I promise to keep the technical knowledge in this book high, while keeping the barrier to understanding it as low as possible.

How This Book Is Organized

After numerous conversations with engineers getting started in their careers, reviewing hundreds of online tutorials, and talking to users of serverless technologies at conferences, I had a revelation. Most of the information produced and consumed about programming is focused around building systems, but not around operating them. Most of the questions I was being asked after giving a talk on serverless were DevOps questions from those who chose serverless to avoid DevOps in the first place. Serverless may abstract away servers, but it does not abstract away DevOps. You will have to make tough decisions when designing, building, and operating your systems. But if done properly, based on the advice of this book and using serverless when applicable, you can meaningfully minimize frustration and time spent, while maximizing your confidence in your systems.

To achieve that mission, you may need to round out your knowledge of system design as it applies to building an internet application. You have the innate ability to design your systems so they achieve the desired functionality intentionally instead of accidentally. This will be done in Part I. In Part II, you'll walk you through the tools at your disposal to achieve your wildest serverless dreams. You are then ready to build. But before you do, you should read Part III if you intend to launch your creation into any form of production.

Conventions Used in This Book

The following typographical conventions are used in this book:

Italic
> Indicates new terms, URLs, email addresses, filenames, and file extensions.

`Constant width`
> Used for program listings, as well as within paragraphs to refer to program elements such as variable or function names, databases, data types, environment variables, statements, and keywords.

`Constant width italic`
> Shows text that should be replaced with user-supplied values or by values determined by context.

 This element signifies a tip or suggestion.

 This element signifies a general note.

 This element indicates a warning or caution.

O'Reilly Online Learning

 For more than 40 years, *O'Reilly Media* has provided technology and business training, knowledge, and insight to help companies succeed.

Our unique network of experts and innovators share their knowledge and expertise through books, articles, and our online learning platform. O'Reilly's online learning platform gives you on-demand access to live training courses, in-depth learning paths, interactive coding environments, and a vast collection of text and video from O'Reilly and 200+ other publishers. For more information, visit *http://oreilly.com*.

How to Contact Us

Please address comments and questions concerning this book to the publisher:

O'Reilly Media, Inc.
1005 Gravenstein Highway North
Sebastopol, CA 95472
800-998-9938 (in the United States or Canada)
707-829-0515 (international or local)
707-829-0104 (fax)

We have a web page for this book, where we list errata, examples, and any additional information. You can access this page at *https://oreil.ly/Learning_Serverless*.

Email *bookquestions@oreilly.com* to comment or ask technical questions about this book.

For news and information about our books and courses, visit *http://oreilly.com*.

Find us on Facebook: *http://facebook.com/oreilly*

Follow us on Twitter: *http://twitter.com/oreillymedia*

Watch us on YouTube: *http://www.youtube.com/oreillymedia*

Acknowledgments

First and foremost, I want to thank everyone with whom I have ever had a conversation about technology. No single book can contain all the wisdom on developing cloud native applications and workloads. But with the intent of broadening your scope of what that entails, is not achieved by only one person. This book may contain my interpretations, explanations, and attempts at pith, but most revelations offered come from the current state of knowledge of a larger community. And to that community I am endlessly grateful.

For personal friends who reviewed portions of this book and provided feedback, please know that it all was taken deeply to heart. For those I have worked with who provided feedback or enabled dialogue about building and evolving real working systems, I hope we can continue to share such insights through thoughtful peer review, or as nonengineers refer to it—arguing.

To all of the editors involved in this process, I truly could not have done this without you. Thank you to Vadym Kazulkin, who provided crucial technical feedback. Each and every one of you has taught me something truly valuable about who I am as a person in addition to bringing my writing from zero to one.

And finally, I want to thank those in my life who had absolutely nothing to do with this book, other than just being a part of my life.

Special mention to my partner and the love of my life, for not only putting up with the normal day-to-day version of me, but especially for dealing with my writing alter ego.

Introduction to Serverless

Figure I-1. "Ancient Wisdom" (https://faasandfurious.com/91), from the webcomic FaaS and Furious *by Forrest Brazeal, 2019*

To begin...To begin...How to start? I'm hungry. I should get coffee. Coffee would help me think. Maybe I should write something first, then reward myself with coffee. Coffee and a muffin. Okay, so I need to establish the themes. Maybe a banana-nut. That's a good muffin.

—Charlie Kaufman, *Adaptation*

What Is Serverless?

Serverless is the idea that you can run a server-based application without having to manage a server. If you have this text in front of you, there is a chance you are already familiar with serverless. But how do you explain it to others? Do you focus on what it is, a new way to run application code, or on what it isn't, *managing servers*? Do you next tell people about all of its weaknesses or its strengths? If your path to success with serverless involves others, and it likely does, you might be worried about how to best sell its benefits without scaring anyone away in the process. You see, serverless is still in its early days and it's on a path of continuous improvement. Some of its weaknesses are here to stay, but they are trade-offs to implementing the benefits and features that you are sure to love.

As the serverless community benefits from the rapid improvements of a cutting-edge technology, it can be a struggle to invent and adopt best practices. I hope not only to instill you with the most relevant best practices in serverless at the time of this writing, but to also help you create and adopt best practices. I want you to know enough of the rules to break them safely.

The first offering from Amazon Web Service (AWS) was the *Simple Storage Service* (S3). S3 allows you to store as many files as you like without having to provision any infrastructure. It is serverless storage. You may remember how S3 simplified storing arbitrary files: create a bucket (the S3 abstraction for a collection of files), then just give each *file* a unique name, and that's it. You don't have to worry about provisioning drives or backups, or the many other previous issues with storing files. Sure, S3 may not serve all file-storage purposes; it does have a maximum file size of 5 GB. Or it did until 2010 (*https://oreil.ly/GtltC*), when this maximum was updated to 5 TB. How did they do it? AWS does all the heavy lifting on your behalf, splitting up files that are above 5 GB into multiple chunks in a way that is fully seamless to the user. That is the benefit of a serverless system. The similarities to modern serverless compute are uncanny: a general-purpose solution to a common problem (that may not fit all use cases), seamless improvements made behind the scenes (that usually began as hacks implemented by customers), and a pay-for-usage billing model.

The term *serverless* is a misnomer, because there are servers involved. In reality, there is no serverless, just someone else's container. The Cloud Native Computing Foundation's Serverless Working Group best summarizes this in a whitepaper:[1]

> Serverless computing does not mean that we no longer use servers to host and run code; nor does it mean that operations engineers are no longer required. Rather, it refers to the idea that consumers of serverless computing no longer need to spend time and resources on server provisioning, maintenance, updates, scaling, and capacity planning. Instead, all of these tasks and capabilities are handled by a serverless platform and are completely abstracted away from the developers and IT/operations teams. As a result, developers focus on writing their applications' business logic.

Less time spent on wrangling infrastructure, and more time spent on shipping features. That is why serverless demand is increasing. There are limits to what it can do, but they are fading away as the technology progresses, and we may see functions become the new containers as cloud compute becomes increasingly managed. But how did we get here?

History of Serverless

Google's App Engine was one of the first popularized use examples of serverless. Launched in 2008, it was too early for the modern wave of serverless adoption. Many developers viewed App Engine as being too restrictive, and that it was more of a hobby offering from Google. In fact, despite being launched in 2008, it wasn't out of *preview* until 2011. But it was so ahead of its time that if you spin up a Google Cloud Function (at least in Python), it wraps your function in an App Engine-compatible package (using Flask) and runs it that way.

The term *serverless* first started swirling around in 2012, in an article written by Ken Fromm of Iron.io.[2] Fromm argued that web applications were moving from monolithic patterns to fully fledged distributed systems with loosely coupled components—which the next chapter will touch on. Fromm made his prediction more than two years before AWS released Lambda. But over six years before Lambda, and four years before this article, the first modern serverless system may have launched. Serverless offerings predate the term.

---

1 Cloud Native Computing Foundation, "CNCF WG-Serverless Whitepaper v1.0," 2018, *https://oreil.ly/A2ehY*.

2 Ken Fromm, "Why the Future of Software and Apps Is Serverless," Read/Write, *https://oreil.ly/vh5ck*.

The Cloud Provider Landscape

You may not get to choose the cloud provider for the project you are working on. You may also be so picky that you only work at companies using certain cloud providers. Right now, we live in a time of great competition among the providers. They are constantly finding new dimensions to compete in, ranging from price, performance, capability, scalability, etc. However, this period will not last forever as business naturally transitions from high growth in an emerging market into a period where the ROI of developing new features, attracting clients based on price, and even support and engineering resources will no longer look attractive, and those things will get cut out as quickly as you can say "shareholder returns."

Think about the costs of storage, and network, especially egress. And sometimes that can be compounded when using external providers for things like logging or monitoring. Even transferring data between regions or availability zones of a given region may count the same as sending over the public internet, and may be caked into clicking a box such as "multi-AZ availability."

How easy is it to click a button and have a database that is available in data centers across the globe? Is that even something your organization would need or be allowed to use based on data protection laws? You aren't just renting a commodity offering. Even when it seems like you are, you are paying for a product. Evaluate it as such. Also consider the "cloud services" that may not fit into your mental model of what a cloud service is. For example, Google Meet is considered a Google Cloud product that is even marketed as being ready for telehealth. So is Google Maps. Amazon offers the ability to communicate with satellites, and to bring anywhere from a hardback book-sized device to an entire semi trailer to your site for easier migration of larger datasets to the cloud. Microsoft offers a lot of advanced functionality around its Office suite of products, which could be important for integrating with the software already in use by some in your organization.

Reliability, Availability, Disaster Recovery

What kind of SLAs/guarantees does the cloud provider offer? What is their track record? What are the remedies provided if they fail to meet their obligations? Google is known for services that stay in the beta phase too long, while AWS generally opts to offer a *preview* that may be more reliable but may still have some well-documented sharp edges.

Also consider how easy it is to build for reliability and availability on the foundation and services provided.

The network between the points of presence could be of interest if you plan on running a truly global service. This may be outside of your expertise and even your area of comfort, but some of these decisions may be made by taking a leap of faith in the right direction and realizing that any related issues will be understood. The best way to avoid these issues and to avoid surprises is with well-maintained documentation.

Amazon Web Services

Amazon Web Services (AWS) is oddly analogous to just being a data center with APIs. This is because of the services mandate at Amazon that states that all teams must build services, opening these very enterprise-y-feeling systems for public usage. This is the only explanation I can come up with that explains why it has so many sharp edges and weird quirks. It's almost like joining Amazon as an engineer to build a greenfield project, and this is the internal service catalog. In fact, should you choose to use Amazon as your primary cloud provider, this mentality will help you make the most of the vendor lock-in to achieve maximum lift. AWS has the largest service catalog, although sometimes to its own detriment.

Google Cloud Platform

Google Cloud Platform (GCP) is a powerful cloud contender that is the closest approximation an outsider would have to Google's own infrastructure. Kubernetes is a recreation based on its internal Borg platform, and follows its infrastructure as a service offering. Or that used to be the case. As the cloud wars heat up, Google has launched more competitive products that are marketing directly to the users of the public cloud, instead of relaunching its internal offerings once they have been in use for a number of years.

Microsoft Azure

This is a great choice if your organization is already all in on Microsoft. For example, if your organization uses Sharepoint, this would be the most straightforward way to trigger advanced workflows or custom logic in reaction to your company's shared filesystem.

 You don't have to choose one of the big three to go serverless. If your organization is using Kubernetes, there are a number of open source options to run functions as you might run containers. Or even better, you can run containers as if they were functions. Knative, one of these options, is actually what powers Google Cloud Run. So don't feel left out if your organization isn't in the public cloud, or has gone "all-in" on Kubernetes. Running in Kubernetes may already come with its own sets of pros and cons that you may want to consider when going this route if you have other options.

Strengths of Serverless

Some of the strengths of serverless come from the change in focus from an application as a unit of deployment to a smaller and more finely grained model of individual functions. You can still choose to deploy an entire monolithic web application as one *function* and have it execute one API request per invocation, or you can choose to carve up your applications into individual functions to reap the most benefits of serverless. These are not the only two choices, as you can meet in the middle and use one function per service/microservice. But doing so is the same as utilizing containers: you won't get all of the benefits of serverless, but you will still get the downsides. Meanwhile, some of the benefits of serverless are ones that you don't want or need, and therefore become problems. Just as every coin has two sides, some of these benefits will directly map to a weakness.

Increased Scalability, Security, and Reliability

This is a core feature of the serverless experience. You don't have to plan for future capacity, other than service limits from your cloud provider and interacting with nonserverless components or systems. For example, there was a big marketing campaign for new users on a project where I was using serverless. I found out the next day, which isn't ideal, but sure enough, Lambda and Amazon DynamoDB took on all the load without any action or knowledge from yours truly. You don't have to manage security other than the controls provided to you for granting permissions, and your application code and bundled libraries. When you have dedicated teams keeping up the servers that run your application code, you benefit from the economies of scale that provide maximum uptime.

You Only Pay for What You Use

One of the most attractive features of serverless compute is not paying for idle time. If your system is entirely serverless and isn't used in a given billing period, the total bill for compute will be $0. Pricing can be more predictable when you are charged for a specific number of tasks instead of instance hours. If you have an application that is used only during regular business hours and utilizes containers or other instances, you can automatically shut it down on the weekends to save money. But what happens if people need to use this service on the weekend? You leave it up and running in a minimal state, and wind up paying for every single weekend. What about holidays? What about a company all-hands event? You are paying for servers you don't need, but if you shut them off, your application has no availability. With serverless, a request automatically spins up the compute it needs if none is available, and you are only charged for that request. Your application is always available (although sometimes it may suffer from a cold start, which we will address later); if no one uses it, your cost for that time period is zero. Other parts of your application may have an effect on your cloud bill, such as data storage, monitoring, and other support systems, but the compute will be zero.

Saving Time and Money on Managing Servers

Of course, you'll be spending valuable engineering time on optimizing the cost of non-serverless systems. The time spent making those decisions isn't free. It is measured in the pay of engineers and the costs of recruiting and retaining them, as well as not shipping valuable features to users! Tedious tasks such as capacity planning don't entirely disappear when you use serverless, but you get to zoom out by an order of magnitude, and that has clear benefits.

Think of it this way: if you can't afford to hire a full-time platform-engineering team to run your code, why not rent one from your cloud provider? You may lose the ability to handle certain low-level tasks, but this is specialization of labor and economies of scale at their best. Instead of you having to manually configure autoscaling groups to provision and deprovision computing resources based on some abstractions of work that needs to be performed by your system, serverless specifically operates by scaling on the real metric of work that needs to be performed. There is no organization running in the cloud that does not have some amount of idle compute being wasted at any given time.

Improved Developer Productivity

Some cloud providers suggest using functions as glue to add logic and process to connect services. You don't have to reinvent the wheel when it comes to the distributed execution environment, queuing, retrying logic, and so on for modern serverless offerings that continue to increase with time.

There is no better example of this than creating an extract, transform, load (ETL) pipeline using serverless. An ETL pipeline takes data from one source, runs some compute over it, and loads it into a new destination. You can connect a data source that will automatically invoke a function for every single write performed on a database, and that lambda can transform that data without any servers or worrying about how many writes the original database will scale up or down to. It just works!

Decreased Management Responsibilities

I have already mentioned the idea of renting your DevOps from your cloud provider when your organization can't afford, or doesn't need a full-time dedicated team of platform engineers. That benefit cascades into other benefits as well. Serverless provides a stable container to target while having someone else manage security updates and patching of underlying infrastructure. It is important to remember the shared model of responsibility when utilizing any such offering, because you still have to take care of the security of your code and the libraries you utilize in your application.

(I will cover security further in Chapter 9.) But you don't have to worry about patching the operating system, the libraries included on the system, and the version of the programming language itself. Your cloud provider employs a 24/7 staff of engineers who handle those choices and responsibilities.

Convenient Integrations

The biggest draw to the big three cloud providers when it comes to serverless is the integrations. It all comes down to the events. Publish a message in Google Cloud Pub/Sub? Why not react to that in real time with code? No need to monitor your worker nodes anymore. Add or update a record in your database, and boom, you can attach something that audits that action. Have a client upload an image directly to S3, and you can process that image into thumbnails without provisioning a single server. Using AWS Cognito to handle user accounts, and you want to send a welcome email after a user registration? Serverless handles all of those use cases and many more.

Current offerings provide a way to have your function code glue together actions in different parts of your system without worrying about provisioning queuing resources or creating a task execution and background work environment on your own. Some of this leads to opaqueness and comes back as a weakness in debugging. This is especially true as it becomes easier to glue together external services into your application architecture.

Weaknesses of Serverless

The most interesting part of the weaknesses of serverless is how they become less cumbersome or start to disappear as time progresses. The industry has seen major advances on some such issues while this book was being written, and change will continue to be rapid. To stay up to date on developments, especially in a space as rapidly evolving as serverless, or cloud native as a whole, make sure to follow the blog or get email announcements from your cloud providers, join mailing lists for relevant groups, or even follow developments on a site like Reddit.[3]

The Cold (Start) War

A *cold start* happens when a function invocation occurs and there is no running function available to execute the work. Instead, a new function container will spin up, and your users have to spend time waiting for your application to respond. Some people keep functions warm to prevent this problem, but I believe in using the right tool for the job. People who are faking usage to keep their functions ready for user traffic are not using serverless as it was intended. What they really want is to instantly answer

---

3 Personally, I like to stay up to date with Hacker News (*https://news.ycombinator.com*).

up to a certain number of concurrent requests without waiting for an additional machine to spin up and be added to a cluster. A serverless function will certainly beat spinning up an entire additional EC2 instance, but for some people that just isn't enough. I will give these users the benefit of the doubt by saying they are just so excited to use serverless that they are willing to use hacks to fix some of the weaknesses. If this form of latency is a deal breaker for your application, then serverless may not be right for your use case. Instead, utilize serverless for workloads that aren't directly user facing.

This cold start issue will continue to fade with time, but that future is already available now. Some environments offering compute at the edge or *Content Delivery Network* (CDN), such as Cloudflare workers, have increased limitations on the functions they will execute to decrease the cold start time in order to preprocess or post process a web request. Think about that. While most developers are trying to respond to API requests in under 100 ms, they are adding additional compute before or after that 100 ms. A common use case for this concept is injecting personalization into a cached page being served from a CDN.

Many companies offering are also alternative environments to solve this issue. It's an arms race. If you need the performance at this time, it may not be there. But it will get faster until it reaches the minimum overhead. AWS Lambda, for example, greatly improved its start-up time for cold starts by completely reinventing how it connects a function to a private network.

Compute Time

One agreed-upon weakness of serverless is the limited amount of time in which a particular workload can run. There are some workarounds, but it may make sense not to utilize serverless in some use cases.

However, this limitation is arbitrary in many ways. In 2018, Amazon changed the limits on Lambda from 5 minutes to 15 minutes. There was no need to rearchitect Lambda to make this change. As some issues with serverless are solved, the solutions will be available to you without any additional engineering overhead. You may have to spend engineering time to take the most advantage of the changing landscape, but your system will still work without those changes as well.

VPC/Network Issues

If your application needs to run inside a specific private subnet or cloud network, there are some limitations. You can't scale to 10,000 concurrent executions in a subnet with room for 254 IP addresses. Depending on your organization, you may be forced to operate in a virtual private cloud (VPC) in order to access private resources, or your application may call for accessing a database that can only be reached in a certain network. You will have to capacity plan to make sure your private networks are large enough. If you want to build a truly serverless system, you will have to avoid certain cloud offerings, persistence layers, or other design choices that will tie you to a specific private network.

Application Size

Limitations like compute time are also arbitrary, but if your application is too large, the cold start times may become unmanageable, so limiting the bundle size of your application is a good sanity check. How does this limitation affect you? One example is that you may not be able to ship a large Java application into a serverless function— using containers or instances is a better strategy for now, but keep an eye out for changes that could enable this. You may also be limited in the amount and size of dependencies of your application, although with the introduction of layers in AWS, there are advancements in this area as well.

Potential to Be More Expensive

If your application requires a predictable and stable amount of compute, you will overpay by using serverless. But consider the cost of maintenance and upkeep required for patching systems with security and other updates. You can pay your employees to do this, or you can *overpay* for your compute to have some of those maintenance costs bundled in. Does it make more sense to spend an extra $200,000 per year on a DevOps engineer or overpay on your cloud bill by $20,000 per year? Spend that money on another engineer who will build functionality with directly attributable revenue.

Vendor Lock-In

Every technology you select will likely lock you into using a specific vendor in one way or another: which base Docker image you use, which database you use, should you really add that additional package, and so on. You can lessen this by having your organization self-host a function execution environment on top of Kubernetes using open source software. But there is a high likelihood your organization already has some level of vendor lock-in to one of these cloud providers. If your organization has already made a trade-off in a specific direction, it makes sense to piggyback on top of that. This may be the case for you.

Vendor lock-in is an interesting concern. Some suggest this is just an overreaction to switching costs, which comes with all technology choices. They liken it to what happens if you want to change from Java to Python, or Go to Erlang. This is true only in that every developer has the choice of making optimizations and trade-offs as they see fit. Sure, you can save a lot of money on hosting costs by running your application on an old server under your desk, or on a cluster of Raspberry Pis, but you will likely choose to use virtualized instances from a large cloud provider because you will have to decide how you want to spend your time: writing code, or carrying buckets of diesel fuel up a staircase after a hurricane (see "The Physical World" on page 4).

Lock-in is something to be mindful of, but not to spend much time on. I will be focusing on examples primarily from AWS due to the depth of supporting services and integrations, but these examples are for illustration purposes. I am not advocating allegiance to any one particular provider, and think the most pragmatic approach is to keep your options open.

If your organization has chosen to invest in one of these platforms, take advantage of the deep service catalog you have available to get your job done in the best way with the fewest trade-offs possible. Learn to love your provider, but don't trust them more than you should.

Complex Debugging

When you have a dynamic runtime, debugging can be complicated to reproduce errors in order to solve them. The more components or microservices your system is comprised of, the more difficult it can be to trace a user action throughout the entire system. That's why so many tools and SaaS offerings address these issues. I believe this is generally a symptom of using serverless incorrectly. Used correctly, serverless should give you more understanding of the core functionality of your systems. Some of these tools, however, are evolving into really compelling ways to find and filter issues, as well as providing data helpful in reproducing such errors. Your debugging and introspection are more powerful than ever before. What a time to be alive!

When Does It Make Sense to Use Serverless?

Many developers are making the move to serverless, or exploring serverless components for parts of their applications. Werner Vogels says (*https://oreil.ly/z2Y5L*):

> At Amazon, we're not completely serverless ourselves, but we're moving in that direction. And so are many of our customers. In fact, we anticipate that there will soon be a whole generation of developers who have never touched a server and only write business logic. The reason is simple. Whether you're building net new applications or migrating legacy, using serverless primitives for compute, data, and integration enables you to benefit from the most agility that the cloud has to offer.

He sees serverless primitives (the most basic types of resources), as superior to their server-based equivalents, just as the cloud primitives were superior to the data center primitives were superior to the mainframe equivalents.

Use cases vary, but here are some of the most common and best reasons to use serverless.

The most important factor to determine your *success* will be the use case. Have you heard people complain about serverless? What do they talk about? Cold starts. While cold starts will eventually be optimized as close to zero as possible, you can build a system that is unaffected by cold starts. This pattern is the same for people who complain about how NoSQL doesn't have transactions, or how iPads don't have mouse support. Although these days, things are changing: DynamoDB offers NoSQL with transactions, and the latest iPad Pro has a trackpad.

You don't need a specific reason to use serverless, but here are some examples of the characteristics of the compute work you want to perform that will have the least friction and most benefit when utilizing serverless:

- Tasks that can be broken up into small independent units of work
- Tasks that either have infrequent or unpredictable usage patterns
- Background work, or system to system communication that will not be impacted by cold starts

Let's break these down. A *task* is a unit of work that isn't blocking, and can be broken up into smaller units of work that would each fit into a function.

Serverless is best used for load that is not predictable. This doesn't mean you can't use it in this case, it just may not be the most efficient and will cost more than use containers (but again, that doesn't include the overhead of managing the containers).

But what about your workload? If you can see your system as a collection of easily separable parts, and you don't want to deal with the overhead of servers for a lack of resources, it may make sense to use serverless.

Some parts of your application will be high velocity, at least when it comes to the rate of change of features and priorities. But then you have the strong and steady workhorse components. Imagine some of the problems you have yet to solve. There are some parts of your overall application that will be low velocity once version 1.0 is shipped. They don't directly serve users, but offload work from the application servers that do. Sending email to users is a perfect asynchronous task to set up to happen in the background that won't need much change to the basic architecture. It has somewhat unpredictable demand. And while you want it to happen in real time, the latency of a cold start is not going to ruin the password reset experience for a user locked out of their account.

Another interesting use case of serverless is the nearly infinite scale it brings. Let's assume it takes 30 seconds to process one minute of high resolution video for streaming. How long will it take to process a 90-minute film? 30 seconds. Because you can break up and parallelize the work and instantly feed it out to as many Lambda functions as possible, you can drastically speed up the time it takes to complete a task. This is actually one way Netflix uses serverless.

Another strong use case for serverless is event-driven architecture. Chapter 3 will cover serverless architectural patterns in detail.

One of the most helpful uses of serverless compute is that it acts as the glue between services. For example, you can monitor the utilization of a resource to scale a service up or down to save costs.

Want to resize uploaded images into thumbnails automatically without setting up a task or queueing service? Do you want to save money on your instances by using *spot* instances that cost less money than traditional instances? When those spot instances are being taken away (part of the reason they are less expensive), you can have a function automatically invoked on that cloud event to spin up a regular instance to take its place. Another spot instance becomes available later? Same thing in reverse: your function can spin up the instance that costs less money and terminate the more expensive one. Want to react to changes in data as they happen without adding brittle analytical code to the main conversion funnel of your application? Serverless can help with all of these use cases. It can be glue, DevOps, automation, out-of-band processing of data, or fully fledged applications.

When Is Serverless Compute Not Right for You?

Serverless will not serve you best when you have tasks that are computationally intensive, when your tasks have a long runtime that can't be broken up into smaller workloads, or when you need additional functionality not currently supported by the cloud providers, to name a few examples. These tasks might look like reading a large table of data and turning each row into an API request, encoding a feature-length film for streaming, or running a persistent WebSockets connection for a chat function. But some of these examples do have ways of being adapted to work. You can run a parallel scan or certain types of datastores such as DynamoDB. You can break up large files into smaller parallelized chucks as Netflix currently does to encode movies. You can use an API Gateway with WebSockets to maintain a real-time connection to clients, while invoking a Lambda for each message passed.

Let's Get Started

It is time to start or continue your serverless journey. By the end of this book you will have learned many fundamentals and best practices needed to succeed in any form of cloud computing, servers or not.

How "full stack" are you? If you specialize in certain areas, how did you choose those areas? Did you try other things out before deciding not to be an expert? You need to know how to manage servers before you can manage a system that manages them for you.

The choice to go serverless, is generally made to reduce the complexity in configuring and managing infrastructure, but you must have some basic understanding of the work you are abstracting away to build a reliable system on top of it. That will all be covered in this book.

Part I of this book will walk you through what it means to launch a proper production system. There will be servers involved, of course, but you won't need to know them personally. Part II will cover the tools you will need to be successful with serverless. Part III will cover some more advanced topics in depth, such as security.

Now let's talk about production systems.

The Path to Production

"Multicloud" (https://faasandfurious.com/72), from the webcomic FaaS and Furious *by Forrest Brazeal, 2018*

CHAPTER 1

Distributed Systems

We'll begin our journey through serverless by talking about distributed systems. Before we jump into definitions and examples, what do you need to know about distributed systems to be effective with serverless? When you develop an application, you have to make a large number of assumptions. Some may be as simple as knowing that one step will occur after another. Others may be far more complex. Distributed systems will tear apart all your assumptions about the environment in which your code will run and how it will operate. When you develop for a single computer, many of the harsh realities of the physical world are abstracted away. As soon as you start building a system that resides on multiple computers, all of those realities suddenly surface—though they might not be obvious.

This chapter will first offer a broad overview to better understand what you have signed up for.

If you do not have experience developing backend systems, my goal is to explain what has changed about your world. But even if you have experience, you will find value here: distributed systems can bring out the pessimism and cynicism even in experienced software engineers and system administrators. We'll talk about what can go wrong and what you can do about it.

What Is a Distributed System?

A *distributed system* is any system where the individual components are separated and communicate over a network. A distributed system can be part of a larger or smaller distributed system. The internet is one giant distributed system. Your cell phone provider operates a giant distributed system in order to connect you to an even bigger one. Their system contains wireless gear, network gear, and applications such as billing and customer information.

When working with apps, we usually expect determinism: given a specific input, the output, and the states and sequences to achieve that output, will always be the same. The reality of distributed systems, however, is nondeterminism. As the complexity of your application grows, it becomes difficult to predict the state of it at any given point. It is assumed that all parts of the system will be unreliable in either obvious or nonobvious ways, but it is your job to build a reliable system from these unreliable components.

Your application does not live or process logic in a single place. If you have a browser-based application or a mobile application, the second you put a line of code in any other place, such as a function in the cloud, your system is distributed. Generally, components of a distributed system are *asynchronous*, meaning they pass off a task and do not wait directly for the result. But many important operations, such as the processing of credit card transactions, will be accessed synchronously, as they should block the progress of the calling task until completion of the vital transaction.

A serverless system is inherently distributed. Given that a serverless function is by its very nature stateless, if your application involves any form of state, it is going to have to be distributed. But aren't all modern applications distributed? While the answer is likely yes, it is definitely true for applications that have ambitions to grow and become more complex.

If you are building a simple web app with a client frontend, a monolithic backend, and a database (also known as a three-tiered web application), then you are building a distributed system. However, many developers will neglect this fact when thinking about how the application stores its state in a database. And they will run into problems as a result. At some point in scaling up their system, they will likely face an issue caused by an application server, regarded as being easily and horizontally scalable, connecting to their database (vertically scalable). This issue could range anywhere from needing more resources for the database to simply needing to update the database configuration to allow additional connections. But those developers who forget they are working on a distributed system will have all of the problems of one, without any of the common patterns to minimize issues.

Serverless shifts many responsibilities to your cloud provider. However, as the software practitioner writing the business logic, there are still things you need to know and understand to make promises to your stakeholders in regard to the reliability, availability, and scalability of your software.

Why Do We Want a Distributed System?

Do you need a solution that handles what happens when someone introduces a bug that causes your database to lock, preventing your main user-facing system from operating? Well, that's actually a strength of distributed systems because you can kill the failing service, and all of the work expected to be done by it will be delayed but not lost as it queues up. If your user registration code ran the email sending code directly, you would be down completely. Designing so that one failure does not cascade and directly cause another is the subject of Chapters 4 and 11, but the resources listed in "Further Reading" on page 11 cover these concepts in much more depth.

Any application intended to *scale* must be a distributed system. Otherwise, you will be limited to the compute and storage of one computer, and your users must visit this computer and use it in person, only one at a time. There are many advantages of distributed systems, but there is no choice to be made. You are building a distributed system. You must learn the disadvantages of doing so to best limit their impact on your operations.

The Harsh Realities of Distributed Systems

Nothing about the network can be trusted. And in a distributed system, messages must be passed over the network. In *Designing Data-Intensive Applications* (O'Reilly), Martin Kleppmann expands on this interconnected relationship between your code and the source of so many problems, the network:

> A node in the network cannot know anything for sure—it can only make guesses based on the messages it receives (or doesn't receive) via the network. A node can only find out what state another node is in (what data it has stored, whether it is correctly functioning, etc.) by exchanging messages with it. If a remote node doesn't respond, there is no way of knowing what state it is in, because problems in the network cannot reliably be distinguished from problems at a node.

Networks seem to be pretty reliable, but every now and then you have to hit the refresh button or wait. In a distributed system, your system has to deal with automating that refresh. If one system goes down, and all of the other systems start attacking it with requests when it is already failing to keep up, what happens?

There are far fewer things to consider when two pieces of code run in the same stack. Asynchronicity can create a lot of unintended effects, especially when unexpected by the programmer. Now add the reliability of a network to that.

To illustrate these issues, let's look at a common application. This application has a user registration process. New registrations go into a task queue to perform some operations, such as sending a welcome email. The developer made a smart choice to decouple the user's registration and the back-of-the-house logic, such as sending an email. If the application was suffering from issues with sending email, it should not block the user from registering successfully. Other actions in the system may also cause a task to get queued up that will send some form of notification. Seems simple, right? Let's get to it.

The Physical World

In the aftermath of Hurricane Sandy in 2012, a group of operational engineers found themselves in a precarious situation. The power was out in Lower Manhattan. The data center had generators and diesel fuel on hand, but the diesel pump had failed due to flooding; the pump was in the basement, and the generators were on the roof. Heroically, the engineers mounted a bucket brigade to bring diesel fuel (*https://oreil.ly/6dHDK*), in 5-gallon buckets, up 17 flights of stairs, in the dark.

The physical world itself is nowhere near perfect. Just because your organization does not own the servers, or can't even touch or see them, does not mean you will not be affected by a fire, a power disruption, or another disaster, natural or otherwise. The companies relying on that particular data center were spared by the heroism of the bucket brigade, blissfully unaware of their servers' potential to be cut off at any moment. When you host in the cloud, you may not be responsible for carrying a bucket, but you still have to deliver your application to end users despite the circumstances. The cloud solves this problem as much as current technology allows with multiple availability zones, which generally come for free in serverless compute, but must be accounted for in your persistence of data, and other services as well.

The physical world can be the root cause of many other failures we will encounter when working in the cloud:

Network issues
Someone may have tripped on a cable and pulled it out of its socket.

Clock issues
The physical hardware on the server responsible for keeping track of the time, a crystal, could be defective.

Unresponsive node
There could be a fire.

Calling attention to this allows us to drastically simplify the rest of the issues we will face and focus more on the impact of these issues as you design your systems.

Missing Messages

Have you ever sent an email only to later find it stuck in the drafts or the outbox?

There is no guarantee when you make a request over a network that it will be delivered or processed. This is one of the many things we take for granted when working on software that will run locally. These issues are the simple reality of computing that has been abstracted away from engineers enough that people have forgotten their existence. Networks can have congestion just like your local interstate during rush hour. The modern network in a cloud computing environment is a distributed system itself. The easiest way to observe this is when using a mobile network. We have all had experiences with apps that hang because they expect an instantaneous response from a remote computing system. How would this affect your code if it were some kind of live or real-time game? If your response gets too delayed, it could even be rejected by the remote system as anticheating logic. Messages go missing, show up late, or even show up at the wrong destination. The wires can't be trusted.

Unreliable Clocks

How important is it for your system to know what time it is? What happens if you set your iPhone back in time before iPhones existed? Or what if you set it to a time 30 years into the future? Either way, there is a good chance it won't boot. Apple has never confirmed the issue, but it has been attributed to timestamps on Unix systems having been started on January 1, 1970, creating a date of 0. Remember that the engineers working on the iPhone likely did not expect users to set back their date so far in the past, but they permitted users to do so. This has caused unexpected bugs, even for Apple.

Servers have their system clock set automatically using the Network Time Protocol. While relying on your system clock seems like a sure thing, there are potential issues. Google published a paper on its internal Spanner database that details how they deal with time for this critical system. When their nodes were set to poll every 30 seconds, the system clock drifted by as much as 7 ms. That may not be an issue for you, even as both Google and Amazon offer enhanced synchronization based on GPS, and atomic clocks for hypersensitive systems such as trading stocks, though the common commodity system clock has some other quirks. When your clock drifts, it will eventually be corrected in a way that can alter the effect of your time-sensitive code. Multiple CPU cores have different references of the current time, and logic living inside a virtualized system on the cloud has an extra layer of separation from the reality of time passing in the outside world. Your code may experience jumps in time, forward or backward, at any time. It is important to utilize a monotonic clock when measuring the passage of time. A monotonic clock is one that is guaranteed to increase.

In addition to the clock being susceptible to changing more than a second in any given second, there is no way to guarantee that all of your nodes' clocks will be set to the same time. They are subject to the same issues of network reliability we have already discussed. As with all issues you will face, there will be a trade-off in the importance of an aspect of your system to the use case and amount of engineering resources available. Building a social network for pets? Those seconds may not be worth your trouble. Building a high-frequency trading system? You may have to utilize hardware atomic clocks set by GPS, as those microseconds can cost megabucks.

The current time as it appears to your business logic can unexpectedly jump forward. Serverless functions, as with other forms of cloud compute, run your code in a virtualized or isolated way. The software that provides this virtualization or isolation can distort time in a number of ways. One distortion that can occur is when your code competes for shared resources, it may suffer from a pause due to multithreading. It will be put to sleep, then suddenly reactivated but with no understanding of the passage of time that occurred in the outside world. This can similarly be caused by processes such as memory swaps, garbage collection, or even synchronously waiting on some resource that is accessed over the network. Keep this in mind when attempting to squeeze more performance by using threads or subprocesses to perform additional work in your system.

These realities can manifest as issues where, for example, you can't reliably know which change happened first in a series of events in a queue. In reality, when dealing with modern distributed systems, there is an expectation that your system may run in multiple different geographies. In this case, we have already learned that events can and will come out of order, and there is no real way to determine the order without some form of locking, which can be expensive and bring its own issues to bear. But if you need that kind of knowledge in your system, you won't have any other choice. Even then you can and will be wrong about which task deserves to have the lock first. You have to handle that in software. No service will be offered in the short term that will solve this for you. Even if they start offering "consensus as a service" or something similar, you will still have to understand the trade-offs and issues around their use when implementing your business logic.

Cascading Failures

Let's say that you, the developer of the application in this example, did a great job loosely coupling the two components provided. If the user registration system goes down, the email system won't really mind at all. In fact, if the email system is serverless, it won't even run (how efficient!). If the email system goes down, the user registration system stays up. Or so you might think. What happens if your task-queuing system becomes full and no longer accepts new tasks, and now your users can't sign up? This is how issues compound, or *cascade*, to cause other issues.

In this example, when one system (sending mail) failed long and hard enough, the outage caused another system to fail. When your system is composed of dominoes, space them to avoid a chain reaction when one falls. No matter how slow it is (it could have been an entire weekend before the queue filled up), a resilient system will be engineered to avoid this issue. You may not be able to afford such resilience in your current project, but you must be mindful of it.

Unexpected Ordering

Have you ever shipped a new version of your code that included an additional time-stamp field, only to find that somehow inserts are still being committed without one? When operating in a distributed system, there is no guarantee for the order of execution of logic split across multiple nodes. But how could your deployed changes not take effect? Simple: the old version of the code is running somewhere. It could be a task server that is faithfully chugging along while refusing to respond to requests for it to shut down so that it can be replaced with the new version of that code.

Meanwhile, there is another change waiting to be pushed to production that includes some kind of mandatory field on registration, such as a first name, as well as including that name in the welcome email. You have a large day of new sign-ups, and this code makes it out to production. Instantly, people stop getting welcome emails, and you now have a big headache—what went wrong? Synchronicity was assumed.

There were some number of welcome emails waiting to be sent out. When the new code hit production, the existing tasks were to send welcome emails to users that included their name, something those records don't have. This particular issue can also occur due to network latency.

Idempotency

Idempotency is the idea that a certain task repeated more than once will have the same outcome. It is somewhat easy to build a system that will perform a given task at least once, but much more difficult, if not impossible to do in a guaranteed way, to build a system that performs a given task once and only once.

However your system sends email, whether speaking SMTP directly to your users' mail exchanger or using a third-party API, it's not hard to imagine a situation where an email was successfully sent, but a failure is reported. This happens more than you would imagine when you start to scale, and chaos takes full hold. You try and send the email, and it gets sent, but right before the other side responds with success, the network connection is severed, and you never get that successful response. So as a responsible developer, you have designed the system to try again. This time it works. But your task that has been attempted twice, was completed twice, and as a result the user got two welcome emails.

This is enough of an edge case that you may not try and over-optimize your system to always send exactly one welcome email, and you may not be able to without also having access to your user's mailbox. But even then, what if they delete the message before you check? You will send it over and over again. A single node can never really know the truth of the outside world because it relies on the network to learn about the truth, and by the time it gets a response, that truth may be stale.

Once you accept that, you can design for it.

It is important to dig into the design to see how these things will fail, but just as important to deprioritize the rare case in which a user gets two welcome emails. Even if it impacts all users in a given day, you will be fine. But what if the task is to send $20 from User A to User B? Or since we are focused on registration, giving User A credit for referring User B? If that job gets into a queue and keeps *failing* and being retried, you may have a real issue on your hands. It is best to design your tasks to be idempotent—the outcome is the same no matter how many times the action is repeated.

What Am I Responsible For?

When you use an offering like Amazon's Simple Queue Service (SQS), or Google's Pub/Sub, you do not have to worry about keeping it running. You have to know what the limitations of these offerings are (how long a message can wait without being read before it gets expunged), and you have to deal with designing your systems to deal with a failure or outage of these systems. It is best to know as much as possible about how these systems work if you want to best understand how, when, and why they will fail, as well as the impact of anything you build that relies on these offerings. Additionally, it is great to see how reliable and robust systems were implemented and designed. Before using any new system, read the intended use cases, limitations, and watch a video from the cloud provider of the system implementation.[1]

When dealing with serverless compute, you don't need to directly manage the clocks and networks and other pain points, but you may have to configure them (network), and learn to build in best practices around others (clocks).

What Do You Need to Consider When Designing a Distributed System?

Imagine a student asked to solve a math problem. Seems straightforward enough. Even if they have to slide off the cover of a graphing calculator to solve that problem, they will do it synchronously, one step at a time. Imagine a room full of students. How would it work if the students were paired up and had to solve problems in twos? What if only one of the students could read and write from the problem sheet, and the other one was only allowed to use the calculator, and neither was allowed to do any reading or writing from the answer sheet or any other piece of paper? How would that complicate things? This is one way to visualize how the components of your distributed system must orchestrate work in a larger cohesive system.

It is almost a guarantee that each component of your system will fail. Partial failures are particularly difficult to deal with because they break the determinism of the

---

1 For instance, you can view this video for DynamoDB (*https://oreil.ly/LFRtP*).

system. Total failures are generally easier to detect, and it's necessary to keep components isolated from each other so they don't cause failures to spread like wildfire through your system.

Loose Coupling (or Decoupling)

One of the most important factors of a well-designed distributed system is that its components are *loosely coupled*. This means that individual components can be changed independently of each other with *hopefully* no negative repercussions. This is achieved by defining APIs for each service to bind to, while the implementation details are abstracted away and hidden from the consuming service. This enables teams to operate independently and focus on the details that matter for their areas of concern. You may see this concept also referred to as being fully *decoupled*. Load balancers do this, isolating your logic from the unpredictable requests of users.

Design your system to be loosely coupled. Find your failure points and figure out how to avoid cascading failures. Do not let different components of your system interfere with the operations of another system, or attach to private integration points such as sharing a database.[2] Teams can still view, learn, and submit revisions to each other's code, but do not allow any circumvention of the aforementioned APIs. If two services share a database, they are not actually separate services. Even if they operate on different tables, one component can easily bring down the other since they have this tight coupling and reliance on similar components. We will discuss this concept further in Chapter 4.

Fault Tolerance

You must build leeway into your system to handle faults. The more faults your systems can tolerate, the less your users, and your engineering organization, will be forced to tolerate. Have you ever been on a team that seems to be fighting production fires all of the time? Depending on the scale of the system, letting your application control your time and schedule is a conscious choice that your team makes every day by not communicating the importance of shoring up your systems for production traffic, and the prioritization of improving upon *technical debt*, or the built-up amount of important work that was deferred usually in exchange for a short-term gain.

An important part of tolerating faults is having some idea that a node is up and operational. This is where the health check comes in. A health check is a simple API on part of the system that simply responds to a request to let another system know that it is indeed functioning. Some implement this as a simple static response, but if

---

2 Or in the case of NoSQL, a Table.

the component requires access to other systems, such as a database, you may want to verify that the component can connect to the database and successfully execute a simple query before responding that the component itself is up.

You must build in monitoring and alerting to be aware of the operation of your system at any given time (see Chapter 7), and have plans for dealing with failure (see Chapter 11).

Generating Unique (Primary) Keys

Loose coupling should be the rule for any integration point. When designing how your data will be stored, you may rely on your database to create unique identifiers for data being stored. But when you store something to a bucket system such as S3, you are forced to make your own identifier. Why is that?

Generating distinct identifiers known as *distributed ID* using an existing implementation, such as Twitter's Snowflake, is considered to be a best practice. It can prevent issues with coupling to a specific database, as was the case for Twitter when it introduced Snowflake in 2010. Using distributed IDs also provides a benefit to relational databases because operations don't have to consult and wait on an insertion to generate a primary key. When you perform an insert, you have to wait for it to return the primary key to create or update other linked objects. This can cascade for a complicated transaction without distributed IDs. The operation will be much simpler if performed in one transaction by generating your own IDs. And the same is true for complex microservices as well.

An example distributed ID consists of a combination of the time (usually so items can be sorted) and some form of entropy to reduce the likelihood of a collision of duplicated IDs to an infinitesimally small chance. These IDs allow you to sort based on the order of creation, although within a given timestamp it is impossible to know the order in which items were created. Given how much we have already discussed the inaccuracies of system clocks, you shouldn't over-trust the accuracy of any timestamp, especially when debugging.

Planning for Idempotency

One way to attack idempotency is to design certain actions to be repeated as many times as needed to be successful. For example, I was designing a system and the organization I work for decided that being multiregion was important for all of our systems. The downstream effect was that my system would notify another system that something had happened. That system was properly designed to deduplicate those notifications. My initial thought of how to run the system in multiple regions was to simply run it in multiple regions. It would cost twice as much, and would be twice as much work, but the request would be met with minimum effort. Once it actually came time to implement multiregion support, we of course designed and deployed a optimized version. In fact, we were able to deduplicate the messages ourselves, but did not have to worry about the guarantee of deduplicating.

Two-Phase Changes

A *two-phase* change occurs when a change is broken up into two separate parts (phases) of order to be safely deployed to production. In a distributed system, certain changes (such as data migrations), must be done in two parts. In the first change, you update the code to handle the code both before the change and after. Then, once the code has been updated to handle either situation, you can safely push the new situation into existence. In the earlier example of a new field being introduced, with a reliance on that new field in logic for email code, it was assumed that no new users could be registered without that field, so it would not be an issue. But that change did not account for tasks that were in transit, in queues, or even live requests that happened during the deployment. There are a number of ways to solve for issues like this, but it is a great excuse to introduce you to the concept of two-phase changes or migrations. If you break that new feature into two different changes, you can release them sequentially to avoid this issue. You could deploy the new field, and after letting that change settle for an adequate amount of time, you could release the second. However, in this case it would be wise to ensure that the email process does not fail based on reliance on a field that previously did not exist. In that case, you could push out the change in one deployment, but keep this pattern in mind for other use cases around changing the structure of your database.

Further Reading

For more on the topics covered in this chapter, you can check out the following resources:

- *Release It!*, 2nd Edition by Michael T. Nygard (Pragmatic Bookshelf)
- *Designing Data-Intensive Applications* by Martin Kleppmann (O'Reilly). I strongly recommend Chapter 8, "The Trouble with Distributed Systems." But you can skip the parts about designing consensus protocols, as it may be too advanced at this point of your journey.
- *Site Reliability Engineering* by Betsy Beyer et al. and *The Site Reliability Workbook* by Betsy Beyer et al. (both O'Reilly)
- *Refactoring Databases: Evolutionary Database Design* by Scott Ambler and Pramod Sadalage (Addison-Wesley)

Conclusion

We will zoom in further in the next chapter, which will cover a specific way to build a distributed system: microservices.

CHAPTER 2

Microservices

In the last chapter, we talked about the pain of distributed systems. Microservices seek to ease that pain by providing a structure and set of best practices to make sure that the development of your application will scale. You may be thinking: why am I concerned with the scalability of the development of my project? Scalability has always been a pain point for applications and organizations that have the ambition or the need to grow past a single team of developers.

There are many definitions of *microservices*, but I think Sam Newman described them best in *Building Microservices* as "small, autonomous services that work together." They are an evolution of *service-oriented architecture* (SOA) to fit the way organizations are actually structured. If a service can no longer be developed or maintained by a single team of developers, it is too big in the eyes of microservices. How big should that team be? That is up to your organizational structure.

In some ways, microservices are a bottom-up revolution in software engineering. They are a fight that was waged by the masses and have arrived at a critical mass of adoption. People joined this war for the increased autonomy of choosing their own implementation details and the decreased friction of developing tightly coupled systems, such as monoliths. While microservices are eating the world, that does not mean you will need them specifically. We will end this chapter with a look into the circumstances in which you should build in a monolithic way, when to build a services-oriented architecture such as microservices, and when to build a monolith that can later become services.

Why Do You Want to Use Microservices?

When building your application in serverless, you will have to choose the architectural patterns and practices that will allow your application to be resilient and, more importantly, scale. The important part about scaling may not be how you handle the additional load of users hammering your site in production. It may be how your engineering organization scales, making it increasingly difficult to build and grow the code base to allow for the same high velocity in delivering enhancements, updates, and entire new features and product offerings.

As I have mentioned, microservices are intended to solve the most difficult scaling challenge ever: people. People don't scale automatically. It is simple for one person to build an application. They know all of the business logic and implementation details of the entire application. They know every trade-off and decision made to get a project across the line. However, one engineer can do only so much, inherently limiting what their organization can accomplish. A small team can increase the output without adding too much additional friction. But once you add another team, communication and coordination become much more complex, slowing down development velocity. A good workaround might be instead of having two teams develop one application, you have them develop two components that become an application when combined. Since every application must interact with other software, whether it be an API or the instruction set of a CPU, it feels very natural to develop software in this way. By giving each team a tiny but independent part of an application, you can scale up the people part of the equation, and scaling an engineering organization is the main reason to build things in the way of microservices. This is the core strength of microservices, so let's dive right into it.

Improved Developer Velocity

In 1998, Amazon.com decided to reinvent the process with which it innovates. "Invent, launch, reinvent, relaunch, start over, rinse, repeat, again and again" is the iterative process Jeff Bezos, the CEO of Amazon.com, cited in his 2018 Annual Letter to shareholders (*https://oreil.ly/Vf5v6*). This process was not occurring fast enough on the technical side. "Most companies, like Amazon, start their business with a monolithic application because it's the fastest, easiest system to develop," wrote Werner Vogels, the CTO of Amazon.com, on his personal blog (*https://oreil.ly/fhFIU*):

> The giant, monolithic "bookstore" application and giant database that we used to power Amazon.com limited our speed and agility. Whenever we wanted to add a new feature or product for our customers, like video streaming, we had to edit and rewrite vast amounts of code on an application that we'd designed specifically for our first product—the bookstore. This was a long, unwieldy process requiring complicated coordination, and it limited our ability to innovate fast and at scale.

But then it hit a wall: these monoliths could no longer accommodate a simple addition, becoming fragile at their larger size. Amazon had to change all sorts of deep dark corners of its codebase just to add something new and useful to customers.

This is the main reason teams and organizations turn to microservices: because of how systems come to represent the organizations that build them. This is the basis of Conway's Law: organizations that design systems are constrained to produce designs that are copies of the communication structures of these organizations. And it is just as true now as it was when Melvin Conway stated his theory in 1967.

So what has changed since 1967? Systems and their organizational structures have formed a symbiotic relationship where they adapt to each other to build something stronger rather than just the software representing the company's communication system. Once an organization reaches a certain size, it can be argued that it should adopt not only microservices, but the principles behind microservices. Teams that are independent, loosely coupled, cohesive, and empowered with authority over a specific set of responsibilities are vastly more productive and happier before they even design their services to mirror that organizational structure. The increase in productivity is a direct result of the ability to operate autonomously and make decisions without being blocked by other teams, the reduced scope and complexity of the component being developed, and the specialized and deep understanding of the business responsibilities of each team.

Increased Developer Freedom

When each component of an application becomes a mini application in itself, each component can make more bold architectural choices for the problems that must be solved and the version of the truth it is responsible for. When using microservices, each component does not have to be written using the same programming language. Some languages are better for certain kinds of workloads. Sometimes a killer library makes all the heavy lifting trivial. Developers are the most effective and at their happiest when they have autonomy to do their jobs. If you are a CTO reading this book, make sure that any new language usage is supported by a critical mass of engineers who can be effective in that language, in case of an incident.

In the same way that you can pick the most optimal language for each microservice, you can choose the most optimal database. Each microservice that has state will have to have some form of datastore. This could be a virtualized drive (some form of block storage), blob storage in a bucket, or a database. Vogels espouses the use of *purpose-driven databases*. Need transactions? PostgreSQL might be the first to come to mind. Is the schema not as important as just storing data against a given identity? NoSQL might give you the flexibility you are looking for.

Issues with Microservices

Microservices create a new problem for every problem solved. This may seem like a bad thing, but it is just the natural phenomenon of incurring trade-offs for each decision made when building your application. So why do people incur the costs we are about to cover? At some point, developing, supporting, and running a monolith will no longer allow for any agility in an organization. Each new business decision may involve undoing the implementation of previous decisions. By contrast, in a microservices architecture, when a component no longer represents the business interest of the organization, it can be swiftly changed in place without affecting other parts.

Some of these issues come for free once your organization has scaled past having multiple teams of developers working on the same user-facing application. It is impossible for one person to fully understand every detail of how GitHub works down to the implementation level, even though you can find open source alternatives written by a single person. There is a difference in scale that requires more complexity in the organization the application belongs to, and that structure, at least according to Conway's Law, will dictate how the system itself looks.

Even without tying yourself or your team to the specifics of microservices, based on my rules or anyone else's, if your organization is going to get big, it is going to need some form of services. We'll look at some of the challenges that will be faced in that quest. This area is still rapidly evolving, so be on the lookout for tools that can help solve these pain points, but your results may be best if you embrace the chaos of reality and build into it, knowing that it is the environment that you target.

Increased Complexity

The more unique and independent each service is, the more complicated it is to maintain. Keep in mind that every active microservice needs to be actively owned by a team. The external world is not a constant, and there will need to be an owner to handle maintenance or defects that arise during the life cycle of each service. In addition to increased independence, those teams may speak different programming languages.

Putting aside the issue of the services being written in a variety of programming languages, and developers having varying experience with those languages, a single request by a user may be transformed through, handed off by, or fork into multiple processes in a number of different services until its natural completion. This natural completion may only occur when the user deletes their account. It can be difficult to track this task in a cohesive way. There are tools that help with this, but it can still be quite a cognitive challenge, since no one developer will fully know or understand the task's path through the other microservices.

Proper DevOps Practices and Resources Needed

The complexity of having many different little applications increases if each deployment pipeline is unique. Imagine if one service was deployed on a cluster of Raspberry Pi servers in the microkitchen instead of in the cloud. This is an example of when implementation details leak and cause issues in production for others. While one team may have thought this was a clever way to solve a problem, an engineer paged in the middle of the night may not even know that this cabinet cluster even exists. While the implementation for each step may be unique, companies must ensure that all the steps, tools, and practices for production are the same, even though the microservices are owned by different teams.

At a certain size, your organization will need its own platform engineering team. In Chapter 1 of *Production-Ready Microservices* (O'Reilly), Susan Fowler mentions the need for a *microservices ecosystem*: "A successful, scalable microservice ecosystem requires that a stable and sophisticated infrastructure be in place". At first, if you only have one team doing all of the backend work, they will need to deal with the overhead of managing the infrastructure and engineering the *platform* that your microservices will target. Remember, the developer experience is part of the shift to microservices; without it, you will be missing the main benefit of this choice. You may want to defer this, as we will later discuss, until your organization has reached the scale at which it can have a full-time team dedicated to *how* engineers ship their code to production. Standardizing the pipelines and interfaces is just a part of this. But it is a significant overhead that will only benefit your organization if it has the scale to need it, or at least to make it worth the growing pains of getting there.

Challenges with Local Development and Testing

It can be much more difficult to develop a microservice when the other microservices it will interact with and rely on are separate entities with other dependencies. Each service being developed cannot be exhaustively tested in the vacuum of running a single service locally. Depending on the scale of your application, you may be able to run the entire constellation of microservices locally, but that will not always be the case, especially when you decide to build in managed services from your cloud provider. Some cloud providers have ways to run versions of these managed services locally, such as DynamoDB, which has a development version that can be run locally; others have community-reproduced services that can be run locally for the purpose of development. Some managed services are just hosted versions of open source software that you can run locally. Otherwise, you are bound to make separate resources in the cloud to develop against, as the cost of these pay-per-use services scales down towards zero drastically, but you will be reliant on internet connectivity.

Much like the interconnectedness of dependencies for local development, this same issue can persist in testing. But another one exists as well: if your organization has one *quality assurance* (QA) environment, what happens when one of the test versions of the microservices is broken? Some other services may have issues testing their latest code against it.

You have to rely more on the independence of each application and that each team has tests to prevent regressions from occurring. But you must also use integration tests to make sure your applications will work in harmony in the real world. Also, you need to have safety mechanisms, such as canaries (covered in Chapter 8) or other gradual rollouts, so that if the new version of your service breaks some other services, it will be automatically detected, rejected, and rolled back. This functionality may be available from your cloud provider as an API gateway. You might want to consider monitoring the health of newly deployed function code without the need for human observation. Remember, in the land of the cloud, automation is king!

It is better to catch these issues before they ever hit production. Writing *end-to-end* tests becomes critical in the production stability of your app. This is a topic we will discuss later in Chapter 10, but some teams are turning to options like Mountebank (*http://www.mbtest.org*) that allow each team to ship a fake version of their service for utilizing in test suites.

How Do You Use Microservices Effectively?

Microservices help us embody one form of operating rules when developing a distributed system. It can help provide more clarity about the "what" and "how" of solving the pain points of the previous chapter. Sure, it won't help you deal with inaccuracy in clocks, but it will provide more detail for how loosely coupled services should communicate. There are organizations running thousands of microservices, and they are only able to do so with strict adherence to best practices.

With microservices, consistency is key. You are taming the beast with a significantly more complicated architecture, as an investment into your entire organization's productivity. But without this consistency and consensus, you'll have a bad time. With strong patterns and practices, you will have plenty of extra time to read all those microservices horror stories on the internet because of all of the time and productivity you gain.

Consistent Interfaces

Microservices in your organization should all use the same type of interface, with consistent rules about how they make information available and how they are consumed.

Keeping in mind that the main feature of microservices is that independent teams own their own destinies, and this independence can only be maintained by having common rules and practices. Otherwise, the services will not be able to reliably interact and depend on each other, and instead of an application, you will be left with a house of cards. Be careful, however, not to prescribe specific technologies that will counteract this independence. Think about how hard it would be to travel between countries if each and every country had its own idea of what a passport should be like. Imagine walking up to an immigration counter after a 16-hour flight only to be told that your passport can't be accepted because the picture has to be on the right side in that country and yours is on the left. Or worse, imagine having two passports for this very reason and leaving one at home! (See Chapter 4 for an in-depth discussion about interfacing with other services.)

Loosely Coupled

As discussed in Chapter 1, you should be able to make a change to one system without having to make a change to another. This is what enables the high velocity of change, one of the main reasons to use microservices.

Keep the glue between your applications technologically agnostic. Do not allow the introduction of consistent patterns to dictate or limit the technological choices a team can make. Your components will share interfaces, but other than that, they should keep all details to themselves, especially implementation details. That way, other components can never become reliant on those details. While the teams developing components should be encouraged to share this information with other teams and their organizations, the components themselves should be blissfully ignorant. Your system does not need to know how Stripe or Twilio work, but you as a developer may need to understand this in order to better interface with them or choose to use them in the first place.

In this spirit, never allow two services to share the same database. Sharing a database allows consumers of your service to circumvent your logic and tie directly to the implementation details. A change in the database can break these other consumers, which means you no longer have the freedom to change databases when the evolution of your service calls for it. They should never be able to access that data directly in the first place. If for some reason you have to share a common datastore between services, make sure the services have different database users that can only see the tables, queues, and buckets they should be able to see (also a security best practice).

Microservices must be independently deployable. That is the only logical conclusion when the point of microservices is to be independently designed, developed, and tested. If you cannot deploy changes to one component without having to bundle it with other components, then they are not loosely coupled. One main focus of the modern adaption of microservices is being able to move fast without breaking things. This is a critical component to achieve that goal. When utilizing the serverless framework, you can deploy changes to individual functions.

In the serverless world, some of the implementation details for interfaces may already be chosen for you. You may have to wrap or adapt the interfaces to match the standards of your organization, or build your own on top of the default offerings. As an example, imagine a third-party tool that helps you trace your workloads as they pass through different components of your application. In order to facilitate this, a request or `trace_id` must accompany all invocations or tasks. This can be a part of your standard defined interface, and lambdas being invoked can refuse to work if the request does not meet the standards of your organization. This may result in failed workloads, but only enforcing these standards will empower you with the increased velocity of development: in this case, the ability to trace a workload through the code and process of many different teams and workflows. With a common set of rules for how services communicate, you can maintain your independence and autonomy regarding the implementation details.

How Micro Is a Microservice?

Here is a misconception: a microservice has to have a clear and defined size and scope to qualify as a microservice. The truth is, there is no "one size fits all" in designing your services, nor is there a common metric to measure them. The size of your services should instead be a factor of the size of your teams, project, and organization; the opinions of the people involved; and, most importantly, entropy.

Let's think about building an accounts service. Sounds easy, boring, and perhaps even a bit of a solved problem. But when a team decides to start carving up a monolith, identity, authentication, and authorization go from being built-in features of the application framework to problems you have to solve. Let's pretend we have perfectly designed and architected this accounts service. Where should a user's physical mailing address live? In the shipping service or the location service? This will vary depending on your application. If you send packages from a warehouse to a delivery carrier, the location of your customers is not of much concern. But if you decide to start making deliveries, understanding the physical location of where an item needs to go becomes a lot more relevant. A delivery service would likely rely on both the shipping and location services to get deliveries into the hands of your users. Thoughtful design must go into how you delineate your services and separate concerns regardless of their sizes. Let's dig a little deeper before we pull up.

Assume now that your organization has jumped into a new line of business and needs to shift to microservices. The new line of business is so vastly different that a user of one product is not automatically a user of all products. Maybe they have different terms of service that must be accepted, or require different information to register. Maybe you have two sides of a marketplace to service. For example, on a ride-sharing platform, not all passengers are drivers, and vice versa. Should your accounts service be the one to mark the distinction? Should your accounts service know the driver's license details of accounts that are registered as drivers?

The quick answer is that if you are fully committed to the paradigm of microservices, your accounts service should just handle authentication. A separate profiles service can handle user information, and another can handle the authorization if a user can see the driver dashboard. If this sounds too hectic for a small backend engineering team, it very well might be, so let's talk about monoliths.

Choosing Between Monoliths and Microservices

A monolithic application is one where all of the logic and components of the application live in one deployable package. If your entire application is living in one project in a web framework such as Django or Rails, it is likely a monolith. These technologies are not incompatible with microservices. But, generally speaking, there are other frameworks meant for developing smaller components that were inspired by these projects, such as Flask, Sinatra, or Express, that would be more appropriate for a microservice.

When developing a monolith, things move quickly at first. Feature after feature gets added on, and even small changes seem to be quickly applied. But as each component becomes highly interdependent, development slows down. Making what used to be a simple change becomes increasingly complicated because different components of the application have become intertwined and tightly coupled. You can't make a change in the target component without making seemingly unrelated changes in components tightly coupled to it. This coupling is normally what happens when an individual person or a small team works on a system that is simple enough to keep a fully accurate mental model in the brain of one developer. Many frameworks enforce sharing of unrelated business logic across common entities, furthering this coupling. This is not a guarantee that all monoliths are complete messes. It helps if you can separate out long-running tasks and background jobs, either using something like Celery to help you easily defer the execution of these tasks, or by directly placing tasks into a queue. It may also make sense to build certain components that seem highly independent to avoid the future need to split them out.

When Should You Use a Monolith?

If you anticipate the size of your development team to stay under 15 people for the next 5 years, and expect to have less than 10 million active users, you may want to keep things easy by sticking with the monolith. If your project will likely scale past these numbers, I will discuss later in this section how to design your monolith for future separation into microservices, which gives you some of the advantages of microservices without any of the downsides. This is referred to by some as the *well-structured monolith*. This may include building subsystems that would make no sense inside of your monolith as individual services, without breaking up the core business functionality into microservices.

Can I use serverless with a monolith?

Yes, you can use serverless with a monolith. And that might be a wonderful or terrible decision, depending on what you are doing. There are two kinds of serverless adoption for application logic. One is to ship a monolith to a *function as a service* (FaaS) provider, simply to avoid managing servers. This is a monolith. The other is deploying collections of functions. This is more the focus of this book; however, we will not leave the serverless monoliths in the dark.

No matter what you do, you will want to follow the principles we covered in the previous chapter to reduce the friction of running a successful application. If you do not expect your engineering organization to scale past the infamous "two pizza"[1] teams at Amazon, a monolith might be the right answer for you. You can still expose the monolith as different *functions* in your serverless deployment so you can have fine-grained controls and introspection over each clearly separate part serving up your user requests. But let's look at another way to start off on the simple and easy route while preparing for hypergrowth.

Perforating your monolith for easy separation in the future

I was interviewing for a small startup project when the CTO brought up services with reliability around a critical function of a system that was not directly user facing, at a scale of a magnitude larger than the rest of the monolith. He wanted to know how I would carve this up and design a service to handle this scaling issue. My short answer? I would not. Their application code was error-prone; with the most compute and least visibility causing all sorts of issues to the core business. I suggested that instead of having bad code talk to bad code directly, adding a TCP connection between the bad code would just make the issue worse. The code itself had accumulated too much technical debt and needed to be addressed directly. So how does this relate to microservices?

My recommendation took all of the best of microservices while avoiding the downsides. The functionality would be rewritten as if it were a microservice. There would be a clear separation of concerns and a well-defined and specified contract between the two components; as a cherry on top, it would be perforated for future separation when it would inevitably be required to be split out of the monolith. In this particular case, the functionality expected to be turned into a microservice would be instead turned into a library. This library would have its own robust test case, its own

---

1 Jeff Bezos is famous for declaring the correct team size as that which can be fed by two pizzas. Any larger than that, and team members are too busy deciding instead of doing.

versioning, and most importantly a clearly defined interface meant to be used as if it were any other network-accessible API. In this pattern, the library was designed to never raise an exception and instead to always return a response, even in an error case. They hired me, and I completed the refactor in a matter of weeks. The core of this library wound up clocking in at around two hundred lines of code, and despite being one of the most exercised code paths, years later, it still has not been modified. This is a microservices-style win without any of the downsides of moving to microservices prematurely.

What are the lessons of this story?

1. Monoliths can be a collection of services waiting to be broken up.
2. Microservices best practices are based on engineering best practices. Learn, embody, encourage, and adopt best services at all costs. You can break the rules, but you should use best practices when deciding to do so.
3. When making important architectural decisions, you can't only rely on the advice or opinions of others, myself included. Seek the information and experience of others, but make your own best decisions when it comes to the implementation details.

You can build your monolith with the patterns of microservices but without their plumbing and overhead. This works well if you are trying to build a greenfield concept and get it to market as quickly as possible, but you want to avoid the later pitfalls of a monolith. This is a certified best practice that you should share with all of your friends. Here is how it works. Take all of the principles espoused in this book: clean separation of concerns, loosely coupled and highly independent services, and consistent interfaces. Keep these in the same monolithic app, and never compromise on these rules. The result will be a monolith that is baked to perfection and ready to be carved up later.

You can even take this further by having your monolith operate in different modes. A common but often overlooked example is wrapping a long-running task so that it can be called directly, but deferring its execution by a task server. If you are using Python, this is usually done with Celery, but the practice works the same regardless. These long-running tasks live in the same monolithic application code as your tasks that are directly user facing, but they will never be run by those servers. Instead they are run by containers, servers designated as task servers, or, now, functions. One monolith, two different modes of operation. True, it won't be free or automatic to break this up for the purpose of scaling or to help a growing engineering organization, but it will be straightforward and predictable if you follow the principles of effective microservices architecture from the start.

The beautiful part of this is that you are designing with the best practices needed for highly distributed systems and microservices, but instead of dealing with all of the pain of distributed systems, you get the simple operation of a monolith, until your organization grows and a monolith no longer supports its needs.

When Do You Want to Use Microservices?

By now, you may be able to answer this question. If you are starting a greenfield project, the hybrid or preperforated approach might be best. If you are building an ecommerce site, you may want to build with a monolith. But if you imagine that one day you will have an entire team, or teams, of engineers dedicated to a single component such as a shopping cart, then you want microservices and may want to incur the costs of developing them while external demand is low. Furthermore, if you expect that team to have something to do every sprint in terms of improving or maintaining that component, then it only makes sense to avoid paying the switching costs later.

Keep in mind that teams-to-microservices does not have to be a strict one-to-one mapping. The shopping cart on Amazon has likely scaled to the complexity that it may need more than one team, or more than one service. The inverse may be true as well: your organization may have a team focused on the "check-out" experience that owns multiple services, including the shopping cart. It is important to balance workload and team size. Again, the goal here is to model your system on how your organization works.

Conclusion

Regardless of the size your organization will grow to, even if that will only ever be you, make sure to follow the principles of well-crafted services: loosely coupled and preferably independent components, and consistency in rules, practices, and interfaces. Empower your developers to act in loosely coupled, independent, autonomous yet cohesive teams to maximize the resilience of not just your application but your organization. Don't forget the inverse of Conway's Law: design your teams as you would your application. You can't scale if your servers keep failing and especially if your engineers keep leaving, and usually one leads to the other.

CHAPTER 3

Serverless Architecture and Patterns

To fulfill its purpose, software must be soft—that is, it must be easy to change. When the stakeholders change their minds about a feature, that change should be simple and easy to make. The difficulty in making such a change should be proportional only to the scope of the change, and not to the shape of the change.
  —Robert C. Martin, *Clean Architecture: A Craftsman's Guide to Software Structure and Design* (Pearson)

The first recorded use of the term *architecture* as it relates to software engineering was a 1959 memo written at IBM. The company was trying to sell a supercomputer that they had not yet built. So instead of describing the actual system, they described a logical model of the system: an architecture.

Engineering and architecture are both relatively nascent fields in software; as things are changing all the time and no one can be sure what the best answer is, because today's best answer is yesterday's production failure. It is hard to incorporate the unknown into planning. The future may involve not just scaling a system up and to the right, but changing its functionality entirely.

To architect is to design the space for the software to be built in, as well as its shape. Much in the same way that a company can outgrow an office, a system can outgrow its architecture, and a piece of software can outgrow its server. So how do you plan for such things? Through the architecture itself.

The architecture of a system is like the outline of written prose. You are creating space for the words to occupy and a logical way for the writing to convey a higher meaning, otherwise it is just a random assortment of words.

Software's architecture, then, is also very similar to the blueprints for a house, even co-opting some of the terminology (software is eating the world, after all). The big difference is that once a house is designed, it's built and that's the end of it. With software, we can keep building on and changing the structure while we use it. That's the soft part in software. And you have to acknowledge when building it that software will change at some later point. A well-designed architecture will provide you with the hard structure needed to support your software.

Architecture isn't just about the boxes on these blueprints, though; it is also about the lines—the way systems connect and communicate. Because these diagrams are at different levels of abstractions, each line is really an interface, with its own diagram of boxes and lines. The interface consists of the messages being passed, how they are being passed, and the service contract that governs the relationship between components. The interface is an important part of the architecture, but it is generally covered better in textual documentation than diagrams. (Interfaces will be covered in more detail in Chapter 4.)

The Role of an Architect

Simply put, the architecture of a system is one or more drawings that convey the composition of a system visually, using diagrams. When you design a house, the artifacts are "drawings" that comprise different views and layers of abstraction. Someone installing electrical may need a different view than someone installing a toilet (unless it's a fancy Japanese toilet). The drawings they need will have different viewpoints and details. The architectural drawing of a security handshake will be different from that of an API request for the same reason. When someone wants to know how the security is implemented, they want a diagram that shows the sequence, but when someone asks for the architecture of the API, they likely want a diagram of the structure.

Software used to only be available with the hardware it shipped with. Distribution methods have evolved since then, passing interesting milestones such as having software show up in your physical mailbox without asking for it, being able to download an application over your phone using that software from your mailbox, or loading an application in your web browser almost every time you navigate to a new page. This evolution has arrived at the concept of continuous delivery. The amount of time between when a line of code is written and when it is run as software has never been shorter. This is why architecting for change and for *softness* has never been more important.[1]

As a software architect, your job is to understand the domain, problem space, and issues that you are trying to solve. The better you can do this, the better you can solve the problem. Also, don't neglect the solved problems that already exist as you start to create your own. The answer you are looking for may already be out there. People

---

[1] *Building Evolutionary Architectures: Support Constant Change* by Neal Ford et al. (O'Reilly).

present them, write books about them, and post about them deep in the comments of Hacker News, Stack Overflow, Reddit, and I bet even on Snapchat.

What Do You Need to Know to Be an Architect?

> *Computer architecture, like other architecture, is the art of determining the needs of the user of a structure and then designing to meet those needs as effectively as possible within economic and technological constraints.*
> —Werner Buchholz, *Planning a Computer System: Project Stretch* (McGraw-Hill)

As a software architect, you need to understand what the current state of the system is (even if that's nonexistent or theoretical), the intended use of the system, the steady state, the stress cases, and what the future of the system may look like.

But what do you need to know about the systems themselves to come up with a plan?

Just like a building architect, you must have a broad swath of knowledge to pull from in your drawings. Architects know more about heating, cooling, electrical, plumbing, and just about any other "trade" than you can imagine. But they are not experts, and their drawings will not be without flaws when a contractor shows up to install a sink. They must continue the collaboration until the project is finished, and because a project may never be finished, those collaborations may continue indefinitely.

The most important role of an architect is to make (or validate) critical decisions about how to enable softness, while maintaining the rigidity needed for a safely maintainable structure.

Making Decisions

Responsibility for making architectural decisions may not fall on a single person in an organization. A technical lead, for example, might be responsible for creating a design to support the structure of the work of their team, but they may have to take this document to peers or panels to air out any issues or concerns and possibly incorporate that feedback into the design.

As we will cover in the next chapter, a big part of software architecture is the interfaces between each component. By designing these interfaces in a standardized way, you'll make sure all the chaotic change is performed in uniform and expected ways. Sometimes, rules about implementation details must be created and enforced for the stability and structure of the whole system or to enforce organizational or legal standards. These smaller components will still require the rules and consistency of an overall system to achieve stability and maturity in your architectures. While this book cannot create expert architects, you will become an apprentice with an understanding of some broadly accepted best practices.

What Kinds of Decisions?

Depending on what part of the system you have architectural responsibility for, this can vary greatly. If you are the CTO, you will have to either create or certify company-wide rules about the use and adoption of technology as well as make strategic decisions about everything from what cloud provider to use and what databases and languages are permissible to how monitoring and alerting are implemented and utilized. This chapter, however, will focus on components of your system and not the overall plan for every piece of technology in your organization. If you are starting from scratch, these may be one and the same.

You will also have to make decisions about the perimeter of a system to support your organization's security goals. It is important to utilize threat modeling to better understand how an intruder might try to invade your system, and what actions they could try to take once there to pivot and gain additional access. An important practice in planning for the reliability of your overall system is considering the *blast radius* of each component of your overall system.

Imagine a user with access to everything in your cloud tries to delete a file stored in a bucket-type system such as S3. That user could accidentally type the wrong command or even hit Enter too early when formulating what they want to do, and everything would be gone. That "everything" is the blast radius: how much damage could an error—or a malicious attack—do? (This topic is covered in Chapter 9.) You do not want two systems to directly access the same database, for example, because if one takes down the database, both are impacted. An unexpected issue in your system can spread slowly through interfaces or cracks; if blast radius is not a conscious part of your design, one mistake can blow everything up.

Documenting Your Decisions

When Disney received interest from a Japanese firm to build Tokyo Disneyland in the 1980s, the "Imagineers" didn't have sufficient records of how Disneyland had been made back in the 1950s. Disney was fully occupied at the time with the creation of EPCOT and did not want to work on other projects, so it made an offer it thought would be rejected: that the Japanese firm would have to pay all of the costs, but they would split the profits. The firm agreed but required strict accounting of the costs, which had not been previously kept. It did not know what the cost of a component was until it was itemized for reimbursement.

You see, in the mad scramble to realize Walt Disney's vision for a better theme park, the original Imagineers were empowered to do whatever it took to get the job done. Because a value of Disney at the time was a focus on quality and Walt was not much of a numbers type, budgets were less important than the end product. But the lack of documentation on what parts were used to create each component made re-creating Disneyland more difficult, and the Imagineers learned to keep meticulous records going forward. The need for accounting created the record keeping of construction and operation.

With new rides always under construction, Walt Disney once said (in what may be the best marketing-speak ever recorded), "Disneyland will never be completed as long as there is imagination left in the world." This may be inspirational, but it is also the reality of modern software projects.

How Do We Make Decisions?

While in residential architecture, a detailed plan can be executed without additional input, the same is not true in software. What you're creating is an abstraction, not a specification.

When you start making decisions, it will seem that the options are plentiful and there is no clear choice to be made. Sometimes it's better to pick the devil you know, but that kind of thinking could prevent you from adapting exciting technologies such as serverless. As your experience grows, you will become more adept at seeing through the fog. Rely on and learn from others if you know this is a current weakness for you. Focus on best defining the problems that need to be solved, and try to find solutions that best fit before making that decision. Consider the future. What are the current and future unknowns? The unknown unknowns? What are the goals and trends of the organization as a whole? Consider the implications and trade-offs of the decisions. Be responsible for documenting and communicating the accepted decision, and ensuring that everyone is on board.

It is easy to neglect the business purpose of these systems, and if you find yourself in the role of the architect, you must make sure that this gets incorporated into the design as a whole. An architect designing a remodel of your home will want to know if the current closet space is adequate. Their job is not just to certify that the resulting edifice is safe for human habitation, but that it meets functional requirements as well. The same is true for system architects.

People will be the most important part of the decisions being made: not just those inside your organization, but the users as well. Consensus may not always be possible. Keep in mind that the architecture of software will always be in flux, and the best way to get things done is to "disagree, but commit." Once the team has come to a decision, detractors' concerns can be documented, but they must no longer be detractors; they must commit to the plan.

When Do We Make Decisions?

Depending on the size and scope of the project, it makes sense to start with at least some logical view of the system you intend to build. That is an architecture! Now write adequate documentation for others to fully understand the solution that has been devised, its functionality, and the diagrams. Remember that the architecture should allow for flexibility and change, and that now is not the time to lock down every detail. Let the architecture provide structure as it evolves to meet demand, but know that for tomorrow's users, the decisions may need to be revisited.

For a system of any architectural complexity, you will want to review the architecture at a reasonable cadence, and update the documentation and diagrams with the changes. Make sure, too, that the changing architectural needs of the system have not drifted far from the blueprints, or they will need to be updated.

For simpler systems, which will be common in a microservices architecture, a single diagram may be enough to provide an adequate understanding of the component. It will likely be enough for the lifetime of that microservice as well, since many microservices are replaced rather than drastically refactored. The replacement should likely have its own stable diagram as well.

In a larger organization, an architectural review will likely be required before a system is blessed for production. This process may be very invasive or it may be more of an open forum where you self-certify that you are doing everything by the book. If you would like to get better at architecture more rapidly, see if you can join these meetings as a silent participant.

You may have to present your proposed architectures for peer review by a full-time architect. They are a stakeholder in your project, as they have been charged with ensuring that your system will be safe for the company to operate in production.

Interrogating and Documenting Architectural Decisions

AWS's Well-Architected Framework (*https://oreil.ly/ZkGMm*) is a method for questioning the architectural decisions being made on your project. It covers security, reliability, operational excellence, performance efficiency, and cost optimizations as the five foundational pillars for making the right decisions about the choices you are making in regards to cloud infrastructure.

Architectural decision records (ADRs) are artifacts that document the architectural choices made throughout the natural evolution of a project. By utilizing ADRs, your team will leave a useful, searchable record of changes being made, along with the rationale and reasoning that went along with them. More information is available at Architectural decision records (*https://adr.github.io*).

Cloud Provider Components

A major selling factor of serverless in the environment of a cloud provider is the many powerful integrations currently offered, and the list is continuing to grow. These integrations offer a lot of power and return for not much setup, but may determine a path for you that can involve coupling to a proprietary interface. Remember, this is not really about vendor lock-in per se; it is really about software architecture maintaining adaptability as a system, as its use case and the outside world change around it. The most useful analogy for many of these integrations is glue: it is a way to stick systems together without much thought.

But before we get glue all over our hands, let's talk about the parts of your architecture that may be provided by your cloud provider.

Streams

A stream is a sequence of events, messages, or data that can be processed after they have occurred, but in the same sequence as their occurrence, which can be repeated and distributed to multiple consumers or subscribers. You will want to use streams when systems may want to react to an event, but the reaction is not explicitly a part of that event, such as processing data outside the context of a user request. A powerful pattern in serverless computing is to react to a change being made to the database. This happens with streams.

Streams will either be created directly to use as a record of events or a message bus, or they will be a component of your datastore to share the sequence of writes occurring without causing any additional load on the datastore.

Streams are generally meant to be immutable, with new messages only being added to the end. Consumers are meant to keep track of their place in processing the queue (or an integration may handle this for them). Streams do not destroy messages they have processed but move the reference point of where they are in the system.

Queues

Queues are a method for delaying work; they are used to decouple components of your system and to isolate precious resources from being overloaded by an increase in demand. They are also a convenient way in serverless to quickly receive and hold a message without waiting for the cold start of a function to spin up just to acknowledge receipt. Queues can be ordered, such as in a *first in first out* (FIFO) queue, or they can be unordered.

You will want to use queues to temporally isolate parts of a process, or to shape the flow of demand to your will. Imagine you need to process a set of tasks every day at 2 A.M. You can add those tasks to the queue throughout the day without having to maintain a service to receive them. Then, you can have a function (or multiple) kick off at a designated time to drain the queue. Maybe you only want it to be drained once it has a certain number of messages waiting in it. You can have the depth of the queue (that is, the number of messages waiting) fire off an alarm that causes a function to process said queue.

Keep in mind that you may need some form of business logic to validate the incoming messages before they enter the queue, as well as isolate the interface and implementation details of the system. You'll also need to pay attention to the blast radius: make sure that one system intended to write messages to a queue can't destroy them as well. (Cloud permissions can help here as well; for more details, see Chapter 9.)

A specific type of queue, the *dead letter queue*, collects messages that have failed in some way and are no longer *in flight* or *in transit*. In serverless systems, how messages wind up here will vary as it is not automatic and must be configured, but for many parts of your system, you will wonder how you ever lived without it.

These queues are useful for inspecting failures and learning from them to improve the resiliency of the system, and you can even fix those bugs and reprocess failed messages. The functionality of reprocessing messages does not come for free, but you can use an integration to invoke a lambda for each message entering the failure queue. However, it would be unwise to try and reprocess failures by the original function that the message failed, as this will cause recursion and other unintended side effects. You can instead use an integration to inspect failures to aggregate and report data about them to a human user. You can also use utilize queue depth to invoke a function to reprocess messages or inspect them, but be mindful not to implement any retry mechanisms that will overload your system as well as others.

Dead letter queues are so popular that AWS has added the functionality to its traditional queues. That's right: you can now even have a dead letter queue of your dead letter queue. (In Chapter 4, I'll discuss how messages that did not originate in a queue can end up in a dead letter queue.)

Buckets

There is a good chance you need a place to store files for some part of the application. In the cloud, a bucket is where you can store an arbitrary collection of files. With the advent of serverless, the bucket can share its changes as events, exposing new ways to integrate. Consuming what used to be system events for your cloud provider as first-class messages is a really powerful pattern for serverless, and has taken a classically unintelligent form of storage and added intelligence by reacting to change.

Buckets have also become intelligent due to new abilities to query large amounts of data, and they are rising in popularity as a final destination for all data in many organizations. More and more companies are streaming data into a *data lake* (a collection of storage) and utilizing new query executors to run traditional SQL queries on archived flat file data stored in such buckets. Traditionally, all data would need to be processed into one such datastore—a data warehouse.

This allows your organization to read stale data that your production systems may no longer care about, but users and analysts would like to utilize. One such example is storing data about orders that have reached a final state (that is, they do not need any updates; other systems no longer care about the data). But your analysts will definitely want to research last year's data, and a user may need a receipt for a warranty. You can still provide this functionality while keeping your production datastores lean and performant. By expiring data to flat file storage, data here is not meant to be changed, but it can be queried and stored cheaply forever thanks to modern archival file formats such as Avro and Parquet and sharding and indexing tools such as Presto. You can now even perform DELETE operations with this method to comply with new changes in data retention law.

Compute

The serverless instance of compute is, of course, the function, but your cloud provider will also offer other forms of compute. For example, you might utilize a managed compute instance for training or running machine learning models, as this is not a task well suited for a serverless function. These can be very important components that allow your system to avoid being directly tied to regular instances.

You can also consume or react to the creation and destruction of classical compute instances or containers as part of your cloud architecture.

Datastores

Serverless functions are stateless by nature and must rely on external systems to keep track of state and store data. This can include SQL or NoSQL databases, in-memory storage or caching, and other distributed datastores.

It is important to note that when provisioning a datastore involves specifying the underlying hardware, it is not serverless and can be prone to the problems that often arise when combining serverless and nonserverless components. You can address these issues with thoughtful capacity planning, throttling, and concurrency (covered in Chapter 4), as well as other forms of decoupling, such as queues or streams. You could even create a stream that is intended to be read into a datastore.

Depending on what datastores you utilize, you may have available integrations such as having a function fire for each write to the datastore. It is important to include and understand these components of your architecture even when they are managed by your cloud provider, especially if you have to make your case to an architect at your organization who is unfamiliar with the new technology. Generally, examinations of the managed services' architecture will be available in video form for free from the cloud provider's conferences, or, if you ask nicely, from their many developer advocates.

Identity Service

In a microservices environment, there will be some form of identity service. Instead of rolling your own, it might make sense to offboard that responsibility.

Appropriate usage of a managed identity service provided by your cloud provider, an internal team, or a trusted third party such as Auth0 can help you in your mission to maintain the least infrastructure. Cloud providers offer managed services for authenticating and managing your user accounts. This may be beneficial if you want to use architectures that involve client apps directly interfacing with other managed services that your cloud provider offers, such as a hosted GraphQL. The identity service can also fire events that trigger functions so you can perform background tasks, such as sending a welcome email.

When you decide to rely on your cloud provider for something as integral as identity, you are beholden to them to implement new technology. You also save massive amounts of time when they make these changes for you. For example, AWS just released support for "Sign in with Apple," which is a mandatory option on iOS for applications providing social sign-on support. In this case, you might not have been able to ship a new version of your app to the App Store without AWS adding support, or you would have had to task an engineer with building support for it if you do not use such a service.

API Gateways

Because functions do not sit on the public internet, or any network, with an open port waiting to receive requests, cloud providers will provide some kind of interface that speaks HTTP while invoking your functions as needed. This can generally integrate with their identity service as well.

An *API gateway* offers features such as load balancing, keeping the HTTP connection away from your application servers, implementing versioning, enforcing schemas, and even handling rate limits and quotas. Your cloud provider will offer some form of API gateway that also can handle identity verification. This may use the provider's own identity service or invoke a custom function you create to verify a request before it is handed off to its destination for processing.

Before serverless, you would generally use a load balancer and some form of HTTP server, such as Nginx, to act as a proxy between the request and your actual application code. Even if your programming language can speak HTTP directly, it is generally considered unsafe to trust it in production.

GraphQL

GraphQL is an increasingly popular way to create a backend with the interface of a single database for applications that are in fact comprised of multiple services, each with its own unique datastores. GraphQL allows for a single API request to invoke and consume results from multiple services without explicitly creating logic to compose each specific combination of those services. This can be an alternate interface to the API gateway model.

Networking

Networking is an important part of any internet application architecture, especially where security is concerned. Life would be much simpler if we never gave any thought to the networking components of our systems (especially since we would be unemployed after either leaking or destroying all of the company data and systems, or both).

For our purposes we must consider the construct of a subnetwork, or a subnet, when deciding on our architectures. Even within the walls of a data center, a request to a public IP address on the internet may be routed via the internet. As a result, it is best if sensitive data is kept off the public internet and is only accessible via private IP addresses on private subnets. You will have to consider what entities have access to which networks, and which of those networks have access to the greatest network of all, the internet. By default, your function will have full unfettered access to the internet, but that may not be acceptable to your organization due to the possibility for exfiltration and the circumvention of all rules and controls. Sometimes logging *egress*, traffic leaving the network, may be sufficient, but at other times, you may need to force your serverless compute to exist on a private network that accesses the internet through the channels and systems dictated by your company.

Depending on your system, you may or may not need to configure your functions to exist in private networks to access other sensitive systems, internal-only services, or the internet.

State Machines

Step functions are implementations of a state machine that offer many benefits for appropriate workflows. Step functions allow you to codify a workflow as a series of steps or with logic. The principal benefit is that task orchestration and the state of each entity is managed for you without the need to handle any plumbing or even interim datastores. This includes the ability to have an entity wait without having to create or manage queues, even while waiting for another component or service to reach a state of consistency before the next action can be taken. Your eventually consistent systems can be abstracted away as a simple set of steps. Additionally, having an entity wait without paying for compute can save money and is a great way to implement exponential backoff, a concept covered in Chapter 4. Step functions may also emit events so that you can integrate them with other parts of your system.

Logging

Due to the ephemeral nature of serverless functions and the way in which microcontainers are spun up and down in a matter of milliseconds, cloud providers route serverless function logs to their logging service. But since cloud components have a new level of citizenship in the world of serverless, writing logs can trigger functions to fire and consume them as well! This enables you to consume and react to your logs or ship them to other systems (usually as part of an organizational requirement). Logs are the lifeblood of a production application and the primary way to get useful information about the current actions of a system. But they are also intended to be lossy (they may lose information), as sending them to external systems, even the cloud provider's logging system, takes a back seat to the actual handling of messages and business logic. If they must be persisted, accurate, and complete, then they are not logs in the architectural sense. Instead, they are data and must be stored that way. There is never, and should never be, a guarantee that data emitted to a log will ever be seen again.

Logging will be covered extensively in Chapter 7.

Monitoring and Alerting

As with logging, you may be limited to your cloud provider as the only way to emit metrics without an additional network connection. You may have other options, that rely on emitting metrics through logs. Other integrations rely on network calls that may change the outcome of your function invocations if they fail before the function time-out. For our purposes, we will treat all monitoring and alerting options as equal.

A monitoring system consists of metrics of different components of your system. Application level, or custom metrics that are defined by your system, are also meant to be lossy in the same way logs are. (If they weren't, they would be accounting, and stored as such.) System metrics, or those provided by the cloud provider or by a monitoring agent about a nonserverless instance, are generally more reliable as ways to monitor the state of not only your systems, but managed services.

An alert is a configuration for your monitoring system to continuously observe a specific metric, or aggregation of metrics, for an anomaly that should notify either a human or nonhuman system. A proper monitoring solution should account for the lossy nature of custom metrics, and should rely on system metrics and custom metrics to create thoughtful alerts. You can react with automation such as spinning up extra processing to relieve a backed-up queue by monitoring its depth. You can have another alert with a higher threshold to alert a human operator if for some reason the queue continues to grow.

Events from Your Cloud Provider

An interesting DevOps case has come about due to serverless compute. Before serverless, there were ways to consume events or a log about events happening in your cloud environment such as the creation or destruction of instances. But with the introduction of serverless, the major cloud providers have adapted their cloud events to invoke your function with custom business logic. This can lead to powerful cloud automations to save money, resolve issues, or even enforce compliance with policies.

In addition to all of the events and triggers mentioned above, there may be even more available from your cloud provider. One such case is to consume logs of events happening in your cloud environment. These logs or streams were originally intended for ensuring compliance or auditing access trails, but in serverless, the power is now in your hands to create even more use cases.

You can use functions to save even more money on your cloud bill. An example of this is to use spot compute instances, which can be terminated at any time upon demand and have huge cost savings. You can have an event triggered by the impending shutdown of an instance, then cause a replacement instance to be provisioned, so you have no degradation of service in a classical nonserverless component.

Periodic Invocations

Serverless architectures are event-driven by nature, even if sometimes that event is caused by a user. Periodic invocations are a way to create synthetic events to kick off a process without directly being driven by a user. This is a necessity since in a fully serverless world, you don't have any idle servers.

For those unfamiliar with cron, it is a daemon that runs on Unix systems to have commands run at certain schedules. Its syntax can be a bit confusing, but is so widely used that your cloud provider may support cron syntax in addition to more human-friendly constructs, such as running a certain job every 5 minutes. Periodic invocations are the serverless answer to a `crontab` (the file where `cron` entries are stored). If you don't have a server running around the clock, how can you schedule execution of tasks?

Patterns

A pattern is like a template that you can copy, reuse, and adapt to meet your particular needs. It provides some additional confidence since it has been used before.

Regardless of your cloud provider, integrations are numerous and compelling, as well as a gateway to increased serverless adoption. Keep in mind, an integration is not just something you take without understanding its complexity. Nor is it just something provided by a vendor. If you have two services that interface in some way, the cohesive combination of the two is an integration. You can also make your own integrations, in the vendor-provided sense of the word, which we will cover later in this section.

In the same way that software architecture is nascent, serverless architecture is essentially a sentient infant. Patterns, best practices, and tools are subject to change. I want to give you the best overview of patterns to understand, evaluate, and create your own since these patterns could be stale if we stuck to specific implementations of them in their own architectural drawings, as serverless is still relatively new.

This will not be a comprehensive survey of what is available when utilizing only serverless. But these examples highlight strengths and common use cases of serverless, which may not always be the same. Remember, the access pattern (when and how it is used) and predictability of usage (can we predictably scale up and down to meet demand) are the best ways to determine if a certain problem is best solved by a serverless architecture.

These example architectures will not all look the same. Remember, an architecture is an abstraction of a certain layer (or layers) from a certain point of view. The sample patterns ahead will not always be from the same point of view, but they will generally be at the same layer of abstraction: the cloud building components that comprise the pattern.

You might use serverless for one task in your entire system, or you might be fully serverless. There are a lot of different use cases, and the remainder of this chapter will provide examples.

Example 1: Serverless Monolith

The serverless monolith is the monolith pattern deployed as one function with an API gateway in front of it (see Figure 3-1). Despite its name, this is a great pattern for deploying a serverless microservice.[2] It may also be the starting point for your first foray into serverless computing, especially if you're building a monolith that is

---

2 What is a microservice but a tiny, single-purpose monolith?

intended to evolve into microservices, as described in Chapter 2. If you plan to handle URL routing inside your application, this is how it will be deployed. Otherwise, you will have to configure every routes to function mapping in your API gateway.

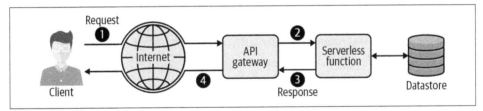

Figure 3-1. A serverless monolith

Example 2: Incoming Webhook

We will cover *webhooks* more in Chapter 4, but in essence it is when a system you generally make API calls to instead makes API calls to you to notify you when something changes so that you don't have to poll and request. You can throttle to protect your datastore if it is shared by other components of your system, but it is best to decouple the incoming request, and your system, by acknowledging the message and placing it into a queue. This way, you don't lose valuable webhook data if your system is not fully functional to act upon it.

The webhook pattern (shown in Figure 3-2) is also used for integrating with chat and voice services such as Slack or Alexa, or for handling other real-time events such as an incoming phone call or text message from Twilio. You can also use a similar pattern for chat, voice, and real-time events, but you will want to shed the initial decoupling of the queue. You will need to respond directly to the webhook with a meaningful message to be delivered to the user synchronously.

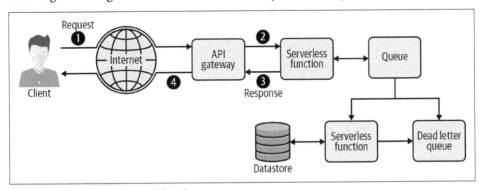

Figure 3-2. An incoming webhook

Webhooks are a common way to use serverless to implement a chatbot for a third-party chat platform. Modern productivity chat applications allow you to create the appearance of a chatbot that is simply an HTTP endpoint accepting a webhook and responding with JSON, which will ultimately be displayed as a response from the virtual chatbot. Serverless works for chatbot integration because the latency seems natural and the integrations usually require little computer power for the unpredictable load and long idle periods.

Example 3: Using Your Cloud Provider for User Authentication

The major cloud providers offer managed services for handling identity and authentication, which this can be beneficial for reducing the overall amount of servers in your architecture because the sessions granted by these systems can be used to communicate directly with other managed services they provide without the need to implement backend logic. Keep in mind that this may limit your options to sanitize and validate input, but when dealing with certain storage use cases, such as storing user data solely for the use of the same users or trusted members of their teams, it can save a lot of time. These authentication can be used with their API gateway offerings to further simplify your focus on business logic. You can even have actions such as user registration trigger side effects by invoking functions directly, as shown in Figure 3-3.

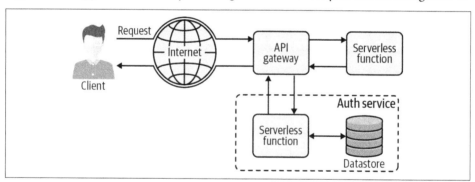

Figure 3-3. An authorizer pattern

Example 4: Generic Background Task Pattern

Almost every user-facing system that is hosted in the cloud will find the need to decouple a long-running task from a user request. Figure 3-4 shows a simple pattern for one popular use case: sending a welcome email on registration.

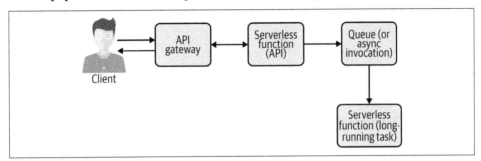

Figure 3-4. Generic background task pattern

Example 5: Streaming Extract, Transform, Load

Serverless is great for streams. A very popular use case is utilizing functions to perform an *extract, transform, load* (ETL) pipeline, shown in Figure 3-5. Set up a function to consume a stream (extract), introduce some custom logic, filtering, validation, normalization, or other processes (transform), and send the data elsewhere for storage and/or further processing (load).

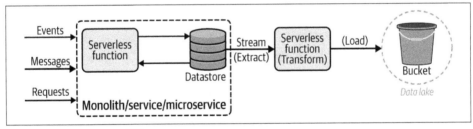

Figure 3-5. Streaming ETL pattern

Example 6: Create Your Own Polling Integration

Serverless functions are a great way to create your own integration between two services. This method is used to adapt two components together when an integration is not available natively by your cloud provider. A simple example is using a function to poll a source of data or events, and create invocations as needed.

Figure 3-6 demonstrates how to adapt Kafka, a stream processing system, to trigger serverless functions in reaction to a stream.

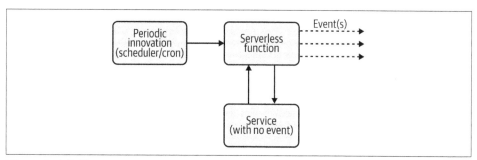

Figure 3-6. Polling integration pattern

Example 7: Processing Files and Images

If there was a gateway drug to serverless compute, it would be the ability to automatically process files as they are put into storage. You can set up an integration to take an incoming image, for example, and compute all of the required thumbnails, watermarks, content sizing, and so on. Even Netflix uses serverless to manage processing and transcoding video in all of the different formats, sizes, and compressions needed to provide a user experience with minimum buffering and minimum servers. You can utilize a serverless integration to have files put in a bucket with one cloud provider and replicate into another cloud provider. See Figure 3-7 for an example.

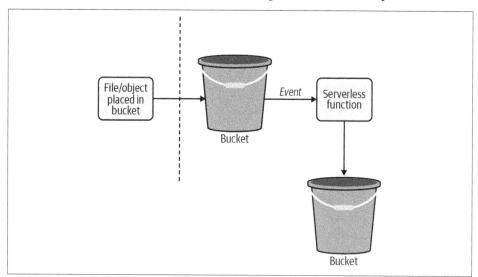

Figure 3-7. Pattern for processing files and images

Example 8: Migration Service Pattern

The migration service pattern (see Figure 3-8) allows you to temporarily wrap another HTTP API while you replace it with a different system. You can put an API gateway in front of an existing API, even if it is external, and route by route implement functions to change functionality or even what service fulfills the request. You can have a function that validates and/or modifies a request, sends it to the original endpoint, and then modifies or ingests the response before returning it to the original requester. Once you have implemented your own version of the entire API, you can change the interface if you want.

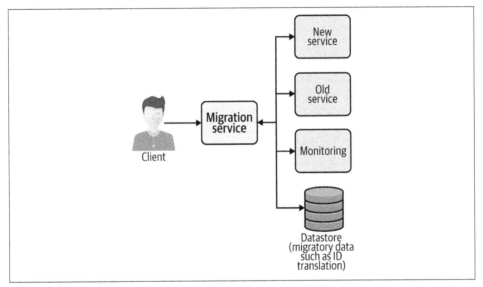

Figure 3-8. Migration service pattern

Example 9: Fanning Out

When one unit of work creates multiple additional tasks, spreading out a message or work, that unit of work is considered to *fan out*. Unintentional fanning out is something generally avoided as an anti-pattern. Some problems in serverless seemed to be only solvable by fanning out. This felt like a dirty secret shared in whispers at conferences until it made the main stage and people realized it is sometimes a necessary part of a real-world serverless application.

Since a purely serverless architecture is event driven, sometimes you need to amplify an event to reach a desired outcome. See Figure 3-9 for an example.

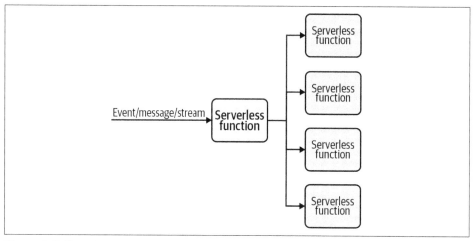

Figure 3-9. Fanning out

Conclusion

Your job is to understand the domain, problem space, and issues you're trying to solve. Properly created architectures provide foresight and stability for the future of a system. You'll have many choices for components: managed services, open source software, vendor solutions, and homegrown. Using multiple services from your cloud provider will provide additional lift in your systems.

Remember to plan your architecture to grow with the software.

Serverless architectures provide many integrations and have reshaped the cloud by making automation more accessible. In the land of the cloud, automation is king—and serverless is the kingmaker!

CHAPTER 4

Interfaces

You shouldn't be uneasy about any parts of the architecture. It shouldn't contain anything just to please the boss. It shouldn't contain anything that's hard for you to understand. You're the one who'll implement it; if it doesn't make sense to you, how can you implement it?
—Steve McConnell, *Code Complete* (Microsoft Press)

In Chapter 3, we discussed architecture. Traditionally, people think of the architecture of a system as the boxes in the diagram, but even more critical are the lines connecting the boxes. These lines can signify many things, and they are an abstraction of how these systems connect and communicate. In this chapter, we will study one major part of those lines: *interfaces*.

This chapter will discuss what an interface is, what to consider when creating or connecting to one, and the most common constructs the cloud providers offer for these lines.

Adopting modern application design comprised of smaller, independent components or services enables you to focus on development and empowers you to make the best choices in how you want to solve each problem. You should be able to focus on the features and the business logic, and the infrastructure should give you lift. But this does not come for free. You have to mind every point where coupling can occur, and minimize that coupling as much as possible. As previously discussed (in Chapter 3), you have to have rules and standards for your services' interfaces and how they interact with other services. But you will also have to implement software using the interfaces provided by other services internally or ones outside of your company altogether, such as Stripe or Twilio. We will cover how to best handle interfacing with software you don't control from both perspectives.

Your service relies on other services. Other services will rely on yours. The key to winning is to design your service with purpose and foresight. You will make trade-offs. Document, expose, and hold steadfast to these trade-offs until they are no longer necessary.

Interfaces: Some Assembly Required

In the scope of this chapter, an interface is the surface area between two components of the application. It is how they join together in order to serve a larger purpose. These components can be internal or external, proprietary or open source, self-hosted or managed. For our purposes we are concerned with the structure and schema of the messages being passed around, how they are passed around, and what happens when these actions do not behave as expected.

The Message

The message is what is being sent between components and how that message is packaged. This may include information about the requestor, headers, sessions, and/or information to validate that a given request or task is authorized. The most common encapsulation of these messages will be in JSON.

The Protocol

The most ubiquitous application-level protocol in the world today is HTTP. (And don't forget about the S.) Remember, networks can't be trusted, ever. They are not safe, they are not secure, and they are not reliable. HTTPS at least provides some assurances that messages are not being improperly modified.

Be mindful of abstractions when discussing or debugging interfaces. For example, when a developer says HTTP, they generally mean HTTP over TLS (HTTPS) over TCP over IP over Ethernet or fiber. Any one part of that stack may fail, cause issues or limitations, or otherwise drive your implementation details.

The API you utilize to issue commands to your cloud provider is implemented over HTTP, and HTTP is even used by cloud instances to get credentials to connect to those APIs. However, you are not limited to HTTP. Many providers have the option to communicate to clients over WebSockets. Your functions can utilize any type of outgoing network connection to talk to other systems. For example, SFTP is still commonly used to move data and even money around in nightly batch jobs, and you can use a periodic invocation to start such a task.

The Contract

Finally, your interface includes the contract, or expectation of what will happen as a result of a certain message. This is the functionality that you expose to software clients of your component, generally via documentation. For example, what should happen if a client tries to add the same email address to a mailing list twice? These are the decisions you will be left to make, and you must provide a human-readable artifact to convey promises and expectations to those integrating with your service.

Serverless Interfaces

Before we discuss designing interfaces, let's examine the options and building blocks available in serverless, and some of the characteristics of serverless compute components in your systems.

When connecting the architectural boxes of our serverless functions, we can choose between two types of invocations: *synchronous* and *asynchronous*. Synchronous, or request/response, invocations are blocking operations, meaning the caller is waiting for the function to finish its *request* before returning a *response*. Asynchronous invocations, also known as *events*, are nonblocking and don't require the request to complete before responding.

A good rule of thumb is that if the action or logic that invokes a function cares about the result of the function in order to fulfill its own objectives, it fits into the synchronous model. If it does not directly care about the result of the function (other than knowing it was triggered), it is best served by the asynchronous or event model. In the asynchronous model, the result or actions taken by a function will likely be important to the overall application, but not specifically to the action or logic that first triggered it.

Some integrations offered by your cloud provider may surprise you with the type of invocation utilized. For example, processing a stream of data that has been written to the database is a very asynchronous action. It is literally a building block of an event-driven architecture. But since the stream is processed in order, at least when utilizing DynamoDB, the actual function invocations are synchronous. This is because the hidden component that is responsible for keeping track of its place in processing the stream and firing of your functions with your business code relies on the result of each invocation to update state, and fire the next one as well.

Automatic Retries and Dead Letter Queues

Sending failed function invocations automatically to a queue of failures, or a *dead letter queue*, is a fundamental building block of an effective serverless component.

As far as serverless is concerned, in AWS, *asynchronous* invocations will be retried automatically up to three times, with no control on your part as to how. After that, you can have failed invocations fail into a failure queue. With Google Cloud Functions, you have the option to enable retries for background functions. However, Google cautions that invocations will retry repeatedly for up to seven days, so they should be used only for retriable failures. Azure offers dead letter queues and retry behavior for certain types of integrations.

Concurrency

An important component of serverless compute is the ability to set a concurrency per function, as well as an overall maximum concurrency across all functions. The concurrency is the number of simultaneous invocations being processed at a given time. The biggest benefit of the granularity of deploying serverless functions is the ability to scale a function independently of others based on demand, and this setting is quite literally the *scale* of a given function.

Why not just set this to its maximum? First, you want to prevent unexpected behavior, so it is best to never leave any option unbounded. A runaway component can cause havoc on other parts of the system, not to mention your monthly bill. The *unlimited* scale of serverless is powerful and will break other components if not left in check.

Also remember that your cloud provider will have default limits to the concurrency of your overall account that you will want to incorporate into planning for the future. If you do not have a support contract with your cloud provider, it may take a week for them to respond to an increase in a service limit.

Finite Versus Infinite Scale

Serverless as a paradigm will break other services that are not set up for massive and instant scale. What are you going to use for caching? How does it scale in relation with demand?

Benchmark your tools, or find others who have. Have something planned to handle it. Maybe you can even use a function.

Your customers will always be the least predictable point in your system. Will a surge in new user sign-ups cause an influx of invocations to your service? Sure, your serverless compute will be able to scale, but other nonserverless components of your application may not be able to handle the sudden increase in load. One interesting solution is to use functions to scale up or down other parts of your infrastructure based on demand.

Designing Your Interfaces

In the FIRST Robotics Competition,[1] they limit the maximum width of robots to 36 inches because that is the width of a door. They could allow robots to exceed this width by being disassembled, or possibly even rotated, but enforcing this limitation greatly simplifies the transport of all robots developed for the competition. Keep

---

1 *FIRST* (*https://www.firstinspires.org/*): "for the inspiration and recognition of science and technology."

commonsense ideas like this in mind when developing the standard operating procedure for your services.

Don't, however, allow these standards to limit your technological choices. A commonly used but not perfect pseudostandard exists in JSON because at this point, it's likely that even your light switch can encode and decode JSON.

Consistency doesn't improve the reliability, resilience, and scalability of your system by magic; it does so by setting and communicating clear expectations of how components interact with each other, and reduces the cognitive load to develop, debug, and maintain your applications.

Because you are going to have many different independent components, such as functions, in your serverless system, having a strict design for how the services interface with each other will be critical to long-term stability.

Services are becoming increasingly distributed. With that distributed nature comes increased complication. As discussed in Chapter 1, a small service with a well-defined responsibility is simple. A constellation of those simple services is complex. The rest of this chapter will discuss best practices around how your service interacts and depends on other services, as well as how other services will interact and depend on yours.

Messages/Payloads

It is important to thoughtfully design both the input and output payloads of a system.

JSON

Most messages are passed around in JSON. JSON is not perfect, but it is omnipresent. As with any universally used tool, it does not handle every single use case with grace and perfection. For example, the number type of JSON may not always perform in the way you expect it to, because 64-bit numbers in JavaScript are not 64-bit integers. This is a perfect example of how your components will have to adapt to their interface, and how interfaces will impact implementation details. While this is a problem that should be minimized, JSON may not have been an intentional choice: it was chosen by popular vote.

Thoughtful design of your payloads should also include creating a standard format for error messages when a unit of work runs into a problem. Remember, just because you might expect something to work and your code did not raise an exception or return with an error, does not mean it worked as expected.

Securing messages at rest

HTTPS provides encryption in transit to keep messages secure from eavesdroppers. Encryption at rest is the principle of ensuring data is encrypted when it sits on a disk. The payload of a function invocation may be stored on disk, but not all payloads are stored securely. Keep this in mind when deciding what data to pass around in messages, and utilize proper encryption on any data that may touch a disk. Ensure that your failure queues utilize encryption at rest, if possible. Avoid logging sensitive data.

Sessions and Users/Auth

An important part of your interfaces to consider is authentication. *Authentication* is knowing that an entity is who it says it is. Depending on how a function is invoked, or a component processes a task, there is either an implicit or explicit authorization component that depends on that authentication. *Authorization* is ensuring that an identified entity is permitted to perform an action, or access certain data. Never trust a message payload on its own merit, as the network is never to be trusted. If the function was executed, you can generally assume the caller has some authority to do so. But some serverless patterns will rely on information about the user session, provided by an API gateway. Never take this data at face value: always validate it in some way. For some systems, this means utilizing *JSON web tokens* (JWTs); for others, it means validating the session information with another service.

Avoid Unbounded Requests

Some requests are not bound by time and use time-outs to compensate for that. As you write your code, don't write just for now; write for future scale, and incorporate consistency and standardization. One such standard to follow would be to never allow an unbounded request by default. For example, fetching a query from a SQL must have a LIMIT clause as the default, both to prevent it from growing in time complexity as your usage grows, and to protect the precious resource that is the database.

HTTP was widely adopted in part due to its versatility. It is powerful but not a perfect protocol, and developers struggle with utilizing its full power and capability. One underused feature is headers, which are a great way to encapsulate metadata about a request, that can be extended using the X- namespace to indicate a nonstandard header. Most custom headers are implemented with an additional namespace such as X-LEARNING-SERVERLESS.

Status codes are integral to success with HTTP as a transport mechanism, but your services should define the minutiae of what each status means. In addition, be mindful of the external services ideology of their status codes. Generally speaking, statuses in the 200 or 2xx range are successful requests, statuses in the 4xx range indicate an issue with the validity of the request, and statuses in the 5xx range are reserved for server-side issues and errors. But not all statuses are implemented by the book. For example, if you visit a private GitHub repository while logged out, or while using an account that does not have access to that repository, you will get a 404 or File Not Found. The application is telling you it is not found, even though it exists. GitHub in fact found it, determined you were not able to see it, and instead of leaking data about its existence, lied and said it was not found. This is considered by many to be a best practice, and it is another reason why the implementation of your status codes should be standardized and well documented.

Another example of the power of granular status codes is sharing that a result was successful, but that the system already knew about it. You may want to return a success message regardless of the previous state because the end result is the same. You may also want to return a more specific status such as 208, Already reported. But you may not want to provide such information externally, as it could be useful to hackers to know if a user with a leaked password has an account on your system. Many times, a website with strict rate limiting and monitoring on incorrect login attempts will leak information about what emails are registered on another endpoint. Never let your interfaces leak accidentally.

Interface Versus Implementation

Just as an interface should not dictate an implementation, an implementation should not dictate the interface. I was working on a system with a bunch of rules codified in a YAML file. While I was onboarding another engineer to the team, an error with that file caused part of the system to stop functioning. The engineer wanted to create a test case for the CI/CD pipeline that would prevent a bad configuration from being deployed. Sounds like a solid use case of best practices…right? Until I explained, "That's not a file, it's a database." The file consisted of rules that were meant to operate independently of each other. A mistake in one entry should not prevent the whole system from running. The database happens to be a file because we don't need a database. A bad entry in this file shouldn't prevent a good entry from going out in the same commit or deployment. It is important that the file doesn't have any syntax errors (corrupt database), and maybe that the data is in the correct layout (validating the data before saving it). In this example, the interface is not the implementation. For now, we care about how the rules were processed, not how they were stored.

Remember, your interface should not leak your implementation details, as then you become stuck on one way of doing things. You want to have flexibility in how you implement it.

Avoid hidden coupling and interfaces

What happens when you share a datastore such as Redis with another service? (Redis is an in-memory datastore commonly used for caching, or storing temporary data such as user sessions). Sometimes, even sharing something as benign-seeming as S3 or bucket storage can break the interface of a service and cause issues for all involved. You can utilize a smart redirect code like 30X to redirect requests to the underlying resource as the current implementation, but having that request come to your service to retrieve the resource will save a lot of trouble down the road if you ever want to modify the behavior of this component or even change the underlying storage.

Lines with Logic

When we zoom in on an architectural diagram, we see that the lines are really more like boxes—and those boxes are spring-loaded. They absorb load, but when given too much load that is not released, they can fail. I introduced these components in the previous chapter, and we will now look at a couple of options for designing them.

Queues

Queues are a great way to decouple two components of a system. You can reliably pass a message or unit of work between systems without forcing them to interact directly, and you can store messages while a component is down. They are like voicemail for your systems! And just like voicemail, they have limits and automatic purging of stale messages. Be sure to understand the promises your queue makes, a part of its interface, when integrating it into your system.

Streams/Event bus

A stream, or event bus, links two items together in a decoupled and scalable way. These components are a great way for actions in your system to have reactions without having to explicitly hard code the reactions in the original source of the action. You also benefit from deferring tasks that don't have to happen immediately as the result of an action but can be in near-real time, instead of causing the original action to fail because of an inability to trigger a reaction.

Designing the Unhappy Path

Yes, it is time to talk about the author's favorite topic, *failure*.

The surface area between services, or how their interfaces interact, is the most critical failure point and requires adequate design to be properly decoupled.

A cornerstone of being an effective engineer is being able to turn as much unexpected behavior as possible into expected behavior. We don't have infinite time, so we can't do this for all aspects, but sometimes it may be as simple as properly documenting something unexpected so that it's expected.

Validating Input

Be sure to validate all input that flows into your components; do not even trust the metadata about the request itself. You never know when that request, "authenticated" by your cloud provider, is going to inadvertently misroute traffic or let traffic that is not authenticated through. That is why they recommend validating even that data to ensure it is authentic. Just because you can npm install a plug-in that gives you authentication, or click some button on your cloud provider's console, that doesn't mean your integration work is done. You must validate *all* your services. Remember that the nature of the network means you will receive events past the replacement of code that generated them, and you will even receive messages intended for other services that may have previously occupied the same IP address.

Even webhooks (which we will discuss later in "Webhooks" on page 57) from service providers such as Stripe must be validated. There is no way to accurately validate the sender of the message using the network alone, so you must verify the signature they provide as authentic before taking any actions based on the message.

Failures

If interfaces are the surface area between components of your application, failures are cracks that wish to spread using these interfaces. Any place where two components are connected is a point of eventual failure. Thoughtful interface design can minimize failure, but its occurrences can never be reduced to zero, and therefore you must design for them in your systems for maximum resilience, and minimum wake-up calls to fix broken services.

Partial failures

A partial failure is a task execution that performed some work before it failed. It is a pain point of developing robust systems, as some steps of a task may be successful, and trying again can cause a failure due to that partial success. Earlier when discussing contracts in "The Contract" on page 46, we asked about how you might handle trying to add a user to a mailing list that is already registered. If you have chosen to return a failure in this situation, it may prevent a retry of a task that depends on this step successfully being reprocessed. In these cases, idempotence is your friend: that is, the same action performed multiple times with the same result every time. You may want to return a success message for the idempotent step regardless of the previous state because the end result is the same, and this may help you when dealing with partial failures so they can be retried successfully.

But this will not be the case with all actions, so you may need to take extra care when writing the application code for your functions to handle steps that may have already completed successfully. You may not think that this is part of your interface, but it definitely will be exposed and should be taken into consideration not just in the implementation, but also in the contract and communicated expectations of the component.

Cascading failures

Cascading failures are when a failure in one part of the system or application spreads throughout the system. Want a quick idea of this? If you are running a classic "three-tier" app, imagine what would happen if you shut down the database. Depending on the implementation of your service, it would likely cause delays or time-outs and would take down your service. The failure has spread.

Now imagine instead, someone pushes a database migration that locks the user table in a way that prevents login from succeeding. Eventually, multiple users unintentionally hammering the login will use up all the connection pool resources (you are using a connection pool, right?), and all database connections will be taken by processes trying to wait for the table to unlock. The actions of users who were able to browse the site begin to slow down to the point of total failure, where all the available instances running the monolithic web app are taken with requests waiting for the database, and any new spun-up instances are waiting for database connections, which are fully exhausted.

To avoid this type of failure, you must isolate and decouple services, as well as section off failures.

The poison pill, or the importance of interface stability

For synchronous events, handling retries is up to the caller of the function. For managed integrations, such as our previous example with streams, where the invocations are synchronous but the overall appearance of the component to you is asynchronous, the implementation logic of the cloud provider will be responsible for retries. In the case of the DynamoDB streams, there is a metric you can consume or alert on, called `IteratorAge`, that lets you see the status of the internal AWS logic handling the stream, or the `iterator`. This is how you know that your stream is blocked, in what is commonly known as the *poison pill*. The poison pill is a great example of the importance of interfaces. If there is a message in a stream that cannot be processed, it will prevent the consumer of that stream from moving forward to the next message. One bad line of code here can hold up your entire system. One failing component can cause others to fail in a set of cascading failures.

Don't fail silently

Do not let important failures drop silently on the floor unnoticed and unfixed. Other than the previously mentioned retry behavior of certain asynchronous function invocations, failures will go unnoticed by default. Not every failure needs to sound the alarms, but a good starting point is to use a dead letter queue when you can, and a platform for monitoring exceptions such as Sentry. Every task and message in your system has some level of importance, and should not be relegated to a data point on a chart of failures. Engineers may make jokes about only testing their code in production, but even when you have an exhaustive test suite, there is no better source of truth of what is currently broken than the errors being faced in the realities of production traffic.

Later, in Chapter 6, we will discuss monitoring so that your systems can alert you to their own health and to a potential degradation of service.

Strategies for Integrating with Other Services

Finally, as you pull all this together into your system design, there are several functions to consider that can help make integration with other services seamless.

Time-Outs

Any operation can fail, but usually it's one that relies on the network or any component of a computer that is not the CPU or RAM. If you are having issues with the CPU or RAM, you have much bigger problems to deal with; with functions or containers, the broken node should eventually fail and be brought back up. But if you are sending or receiving data over the network, or even reading a file from local storage, you will want to be mindful of time-outs.

Computers are very obedient. If you tell the computer to fetch a piece of data over the network from an unresponsive system, by default, the computer will wait forever! Imagine sending your dog outside to fetch the paper, but the newspaper goes out of business. Your dog will sit outside obediently, waiting forever. You would be surprised how bad the default settings for time-outs are in many popular languages and libraries, or even in the kernel level networking implementation.

Luckily, serverless functions have an inherent time-out by default. If you have a function that is a discrete and retriable unit of work and it is OK for it to partially fail and be retried, boom, you now have time-outs! But when and where should you use time-outs? The short answer is: always and everywhere.

Luckily, in the world of functions, there is a shortcut. If your function does one thing but takes a couple of network connections to get it done, you can set a time-out on your function. In fact, you have to. A time-out that is applied only to the connection will not protect you against a very slow but active response trickling in over the network. But, let's say you have a one-minute time-out on your function. If you want to get a lot of HTTP requests done in a function invocation, you want to set a reasonable time-out on each of those requests. Check with the library you are using and its defaults. Some libraries have no time-outs by default. Some have multiple time-outs you can set, and for good reason. There will likely be a time-out for a connection to be established and a time-out for the maximum time elapsed while waiting for packets from a server, as well as an overall time-out. A connection may be established quickly, and the server may consistently respond with additional information, but that may not be enough to prevent the request from taking too long.

Be mindful of the service limits and time-outs when designing your time-outs. Keep in mind that Amazon API Gateway, for example, has a maximum 29-second time-out. Your users will get a 502 response if your lambda takes 60 seconds. Your lambda will think everything went great, and your user will think it didn't work at all. The user will retry and you will get stuck performing the same work twice, then they won't think it works, so they will try again. Adjust your time-outs to coordinate with your services' time-outs.

Retries

Retrying work has an inherent balance to it. Retry too soon, too often, or too many times, and your attempt to make sure one unit of work gets done can quickly prevent any work from being done throughout the whole system.

An incurable, or *terminal*, error is one that has no chance of a successful outcome if retried. In reality, it may just be a temporary condition where the chance of a successful outcome is close enough to zero to round down. Depending on the observer, or designer, of the system, you can determine if an error that is likely to succeed eventually if retried should be considered terminal in the current situation. A simple example would be a lambda with a time-out limit of 60 seconds trying to access a crashed system that takes at least 5 minutes to recover. Sure, the error itself is not terminal, but given all the parameters available, it has a 0% chance of succeeding. But, that does not mean the work should not be retried. Even if that unit of work get retried until its natural exhaustion into a failure queue, as soon as it gets there, the other system may be up and running and is no longer terminal. You should plan for how to inspect and/or retry failures from your failure queues. If you just open the floodgates and reprocess the entire failure queue against a service that is recovering to full health and handling the backlog of retries from other components, you can easily cause it to fail again. By coordinating your systems with those you work with, you'll be better able to prevent bigger, scarier failures.

Exponential Backoff

Exponential backoff is the strategy of increasing the amount of time between retries exponentially. It prevents a component that is already struggling from performing a task from being overwhelmed with retries. Instead, by using an exponentially increasing delay, a number of distributed components can coalesce on a retry strategy without any coordination.

This is useful for any type of network-based request that can fail and should be retried. You can use it for connecting to your database, interacting with third-party APIs, or even retrying failures due to service or rate limits.

Webhooks

Webhooks are the name for an incoming HTTP request coming from the third-party API to an endpoint you register with them. REST APIs are not bidirectional. So when utilizing a popular API such as Stripe, they will utilize webhooks to give you updates on changes, so you do not have to poll for updates. The `interface` for the webhook, or the schema and behavior it is expected to implement, is defined by the third party.

An external service such as Stripe will send you very important webhooks, such as a failure to renew a subscription, or even a chargeback.

Now let's think about this in the legacy world. Imagine your payment processor called you with the fact that a user's payment bounced. Would you put them on hold while you go and figure out what you are supposed to do with that information? Or do you write it down, maybe verify that you have the information correct (and verify the identity/authenticity of the information), save it somewhere important, and tell them that you received it? They don't care what you do with that information; that's outside the scope of their job. Their job is just to tell you. Your job is to faithfully receive that information and make sure something happens as a result. Anytime you want to take a synchronous action and make it asynchronous, this works too.

Tight coupling in your applications can cause cascading failures. These can even happen across applications. You may operate a SaaS offering that delivers webhooks to other applications across the internet. If they tightly couple that HTTP request to their database, an influx of traffic can cause an outage. It's more common than you would think. Decouple anything and everything you can.

In this case, take in an HTTP request through an API gateway to a function invocation. Validate the payload as valid and authentic, and then throw it into a queue, stream, or a messaging bus. Return the appropriate HTTP status code for the payload to the sender of the webhook. This is very important because it helps you in other ways too…let's say your database is down. The sender of the webhook may not care at all. You give them a 5xx status code, so they faithfully retry. Now, those retries are slowly starting to build up a DoS attack on your systems since they promised you delivery of these messages and retries. Instead, if some other service is down, you can just buffer up all the work and pick it back up when it matters.

Evaluating External Services

If you have the luxury of choosing or recommending services to integrate with, and you likely do if you are reading this book, search on the internet for other developers complaining about what that other service can't do. What issues are they having? How many issues do they have open on their GitHub? What are they searching for on Stack Overflow about that system? How many migrated to a competitor after they hit some serious traffic or issue?

Choose great APIs

Choose a service with great APIs. Look for a clean abstraction around difficult processes you don't want to manage. Then, if for some reason in the future they can no longer facilitate your use case, you can still use the API you integrated with and make your own implementation. You don't have to be stuck with their service, but you'll save time by sticking with their API.

Read their docs

Read (or scan) all of the docs before implementing or choosing a service. Look for the trade-offs they had to make. What are the limitations? Kick the tires; read about things even if you don't yet know what you want to do with them. Maybe you will get inspired. Maybe you will uncover some hidden knowledge. Maybe you will find out that in order to get feature x to work, you really need to do action y. (We will talk about documenting your service with a runbook in Chapter 11.)

Rate Limits

The services you interface with likely have rate limits, so in addition to the consideration of using rate limits with your own interfaces, you should consider how to be a polite user of rate limits. Just because there are rate limits does not mean you have to brute force API requests until they are successful. Use concurrency limits for functions that talk to rate-limited services, and remember to allocate that rate limit across all the functions that interact with that service, and across regions, if you are using multiple regions. If you are allowed to perform 100 requests per second, and you are in 2 regions, you should limit concurrency to 50 in each region. Also, regardless of this safeguard, utilize retry mechanisms such as exponential backoff to safely retry when you do encounter a limit.

Conclusion

When designing your system, don't just think about the boxes—think about the lines too, the interfaces. Ultimately, the choices you make for your interfaces will reflect the culture and norms of your engineering organization, but the encoding and transport will likely be some form of JSON over HTTP. Never trust any message based on the assumption that it must be valid if you were able to receive it. Just as you may push an error to production, so might the network team at your cloud provider. Last but not least, always plan for errors and failures, and plan how to minimize the impact of preventable issues.

Congratulations! You now have the basic system design information needed to get started with serverless.

PART II

The Tools

"Sandbox" (https://faasandfurious.com/128), from the webcomic FaaS and Furious *by Forrest Brazeal, 2020*

CHAPTER 5

The Serverless Framework

Now that you have learned the basic concepts to launch your project into the cloud, let's discuss the basics of packaging, deploying, and supporting resources. Even if you are not planning to use the Serverless Framework, you should read this chapter to understand the basics of configuring cloud infrastructure. The Serverless Framework serves as a convenient abstraction to illustrate these concepts, and it may provide you with a lot of value if you can use it for your project.

The Serverless Framework allows for a system or application with a simple configuration file that configures the framework and creates the cloud infrastructure dependencies described in the file. Using the Serverless Framework, you can easily deploy a simple project, or a complex constellation of services. In this chapter, we will cover the basics of the open source components of the Serverless Framework, how to set up a simple project, how to find sample projects, and all of the basics you need to use the framework effectively. Later chapters will guide you through the other tools you will need to get to a stable production environment. Note that the examples in this chapter are specific to AWS, but the concepts will apply to all cloud providers. If you intend to run your functions inside Kubernetes, you may still find this tool to be useful, but the concepts around infrastructure will not directly translate. If you are using Kubernetes, this book assumes that you, or another team in your organization, already understand and can configure your infrastructure.

A serverless system comprised of only functions will not provide a comprehensive application. Living in the cloud requires combining multiple offerings from a cloud provider to create a cohesive application. Infrastructure is the collection of resources comprising your application. Even without servers, your projects may have other resources that require at least some setup and management over the course of their operational service. While you could access the dashboard of your cloud provider to set up infrastructure and make changes, there is a correct, more efficient way.

Modern applications utilize the notion of *infrastructure as code*, an important automation technique where you control your infrastructure using only configuration, code, and automated processes. Following this principle ensures that the infrastructure is as expected, changes are treated like code with the use of source control (such as Git), and changes are peer reviewed and auditable.

While you may be extremely comfortable writing application code, setting up such operational processes for the first time can be intimidating. If you have chosen serverless to focus more on adding value and less on the logistics of operation, the Serverless Framework can help not only with your application code, but for managing your infrastructure. It enables you to create, manage, deploy, test, and prod your infrastructure in a way that for many smaller projects would only require a simple configuration file. Much like relying on a web framework such as Django or Express simplifies application development, the Serverless Framework will help simplify your infrastructure. Also, just like the library of libraries intended for those frameworks, serverless has an evolving ecosystem of plug-ins that simplify common operations and patterns so that you can stay heads down on your code, and not on the code shipping your code.

Note that vendor offerings in the serverless space are rapidly evolving and highly competitive. My goal here is not to make choices for you but to empower you to make choices for yourself. It's the cornerstone of success in engineering—and in life. Thus, I will stay agnostic to vendors as much as possible throughout this chapter. In that spirit, when I mention the Serverless Framework, I mean the open source tool, not the additional proprietary offerings.

Why Use the Serverless Framework?

There are many reasons to add a framework or tool such as the Serverless Framework into your workflow. First and foremost, by using such a tool, you are making the wise decision to treat your infrastructure as code. There are many ways to manage your infrastructure, but only automation will allow you to scale. A change to infrastructure performed manually, via a dashboard or even a command-line tool, is similar to adding a zip tie or piece of duct tape to modern factory equipment: it has no clear purpose, it is subject to future failure, and it will surprise the next person who has to deal with the problem. Even worse, in the cloud, deployments may reverse manual changes, or fail due to them. Every rule has an exception, and in an urgent response to an incident, you may want to make manual changes first (while keeping a log), and then undo or codify those changes after the fact. (In addition to updating documentation and publishing a postmortem, of course.)

Using a framework forces you to follow a certain set of rules or practices in order to achieve the desired functionality of that framework. Sometimes that means changing the way your system works to fit into a set of rules you don't have control over, but other times it means saving hours and hours of time by doing things in a way that is widely known to work.

Additionally, when using a tool like the Serverless Framework, you are benefiting from the wisdom of the crowd, which can be especially helpful when you're just starting out. The solutions you find can be extremely timely, as when a change elsewhere causes problems for anyone using a Serverless Framework. Because you're all experiencing the same issue, the likelihood that a solution will be found quickly and shared is extremely high. You can give back by sharing your own solutions. And because tools that support plug-ins can allow you to share a solution without sharing proprietary company code, everyone is happy.

Even when I first started using the Serverless Framework in 2016, I was surprised by the quality and structure of its documentation. Usually, I was not the first person to find an issue as some new service or change was made in the world of cloud providers. I wasn't always able to find an answer immediately; however, when I did encounter an issue, there was usually some form of thoughtful discussion of why an issue was occurring and some suggestions for a remedy. This is a much better starting point than just finding what is purported to be the answer for everyone. Many times, the community had created a plug-in to solve the pain point or add support for some new feature being offered by the cloud provider.

Using the Serverless Framework can be a great way to simplify and standardize the configuration for your many serverless microservices, if that is the route you intend to take.

When the Serverless Framework Isn't for You

Using a framework forces you into a specific way of thinking. However, that way of thinking could be incompatible with the problems you are trying to solve and the methods you are trying to use.

You do not have to use the Serverless Framework to make your project serverless. Depending on the nature of your application and the cloud provider you are planning to target, it may be simpler to use another tool, such as the one provided by the cloud provider.

There is no perfect one-size-fits-all tool, as evidenced by the growing number of plug-ins for small but common oversights in the Serverless Framework. Creating a dead letter queue, for example, which is just a checkbox on the AWS dashboard, requires the installation of a plug-in when using the Serverless Framework. Also, plug-ins must be written in JavaScript, or a language that runs as JavaScript (such as TypeScript).

Finally, if your organization has already gone all in on some other tool or workflow, and that workflow cannot utilize the deployment or packaging methods of serverless, this may not be the right tool for you.

AWS Is the Only First-Class Citizen

One caveat: just as AWS is the market share leader in the cloud as of this writing, it's also the leader in the community and therefore documentation, features, and plug-ins in relation to the Serverless Framework. The other cloud providers included in this book, and all of the Kubernetes-based offerings, require a plug-in to function.

AWS CloudFormation Is Not Perfect

Even on AWS, the Serverless Framework is not always empowered to utilize the latest and greatest. Under the hood, your *serverless.yml* file will become the CloudFormation template. CloudFormation does not have full feature parity and availability with the AWS dashboard, API, and command-line tools. Something as simple as tagging an SQS queue, which may be required by your organization, might trail months after the ability to do so via an alternate method.

In addition, some tools for describing infrastructure as code document the steady state. These systems will actively make changes to bring you to the desired steady state. If you create an extra instance of something in an autoscaling group, for example, it will destroy one of them to reach the intended number of instances.

CloudFormation, the underlying infrastructure management of the Serverless Framework when using AWS, does not operate that way.

For example, assume you have a *CloudWatch Events* timer, which is a simple way to invoke a function on a given schedule. If you have it configured as `enabled` in your *serverless.yml* file, and you `disable` it using the AWS API or dashboard, the next time you deploy your serverless project, it will still be disabled.

Relying on Strangers for Your Infrastructure

Using solutions from other developers who do not know your specific infrastructure is not without risks. You're trusting their advice on critical components of your system and the permissions to spin up costly infrastructure.

For example, when someone shows how simple it is to do something, it may be simple for a great reason: it's wrong, or it doesn't take into account the complexity of the real world. Consider all the projects that suggest how to "safely" store your credentials, such as your database password. Don't be afraid to question the code and examples you find on the internet; many of them are just marketing to get people to try a tool by showing how simple it is. Ask coworkers or other friends to take a look as well. (I'll address credential storage in further detail in Chapter 9.)

Additionally, don't deploy random sample projects from the internet to your organization's production accounts. Make a personal account, or have your company create a sandbox account for learning.

Finally, take care with letting code run on your computer, especially code that can affect your company financially. People actively look for leaked credentials on websites such as GitHub so that hackers can spin up costly cloud infrastructure to do things as relatively innocuous as mine for cryptocurrency and leave you stuck with the bill (and the inefficiency of overpaying to mine) or as damaging as doing that while infiltrating and compromising your organization's cloud resources and its treasure trove of data.

It is not just bad projects that get hacked; good projects get hacked too.

Personally, I like to avoid using `sudo` to install software—that is, running commands as `root` as much as possible. So I install my development languages in the user space; on macOS this is done with `brew install`.[1] This allows you to `pip install` or `npm install` without having to run as root. This can also be achieved by explicitly installing packages in the user space (`pip install --user`), or using a virtual environment (`virtualenv` in Python), or using other project dependency management tools such as `npm` to keep requirements contained inside a specific project folder. All of these approaches limit the permissions of potentially malicious packages, but all dependencies should be vetted before even trying them out on your local machine.

It is difficult to get into the specifics of what makes a specific sample code, blog post, or set of instructions wrong for your adoption. My hope is that by the end of this book, you will be equipped with the information, understanding, and discipline of being mindful of such things. But it is important to remember that the context will dictate how strict or lax your security posture needs to be. And let us be thankful for the people who spent their time sharing examples and knowledge and not judge them for what they may not know, or may have omitted for the sake of simplicity.

What to Know Before You Start

To simplify the instructions and examples later in this chapter, I would first like to review a couple of topics that you may not already be familiar with.

---

[1] Your package manager may support installing a language outside of the expected default system directories.

YAML

YAML has seen elevated popularity for configurations due to its clean syntax that produces cleaner *diffs* or changes for your Git repository, and ability to have comments.

The aptly named *Yet Another Markup Language* (YAML) is not a replacement for HTML but is instead an alternative to using JSON or other formats to store data such as a configuration file in a human readable and machine readable format. If that sounds like JSON to you, you're right: the creators of YAML have included JSON to be syntactically correct YAML. That certainly makes switching to YAML a cinch, as you don't have to change any of the files to a new format. But that is not the type of YAML syntax you will likely see in the real world; instead it looks like Example 5-1.

Example 5-1. Example of YAML syntax

```
key: value
an_array:
  - something
  - something else
a_dictionary:
  a_string: blah
  one_more_string: No quotes needed most of the time
  another_string: "This time in quotes"
  a_boolean: Yes # Comment to inform you that a string is not always a string
  another_boolean: true
  a_number: 4
  another_number: 3.14
  this_is_not_a_number: 2.7.12 # it is a string!
```

However, there is no perfect format, and YAML is no exception. There are some sharp edges that can get you, and it is worth doing some reading about YAML best practices. The main criticism is how the advanced functionality of YAML can lead to unexpected results for those not fully familiar with its behavior.

Example 5-2 is the equivalent of Example 5-1 in JSON, but notice one hugely popular feature of YAML that is missing in JSON: comments!

Example 5-2. Example of JSON syntax

```
{
  "key": "value",
  "an_array": [
    "something",
    "something else"
  ],
  "a_dictionary": {
    "a_string": "blah",
```

```
    "one_more_string": "No quotes needed most of the time",
    "another_string": "This time in quotes",
    "a_boolean": true,
    "another_boolean": true,
    "a_number": 4,
    "another_number": 3.14,
    "this_is_not_a_number": "2.7.12"
  }
}
```

If this is your first time encountering YAML, read the docs to better understand how it is parsed and avoid any mistakes.

Node.js

If you use the Serverless Framework, you will have to understand the most basic parts of Node.js's package manager, NPM.

The *package.json* file is used both for packages and libraries being published to the NPM repository, or for private projects. For a serverless project that relies on plug-ins, you will need to have this file, as well as a *package-lock.json* file. The lockfile, as it is known, is a common pattern to specify the exact versions of dependencies being used, to lock them in time, and to make sure your builds and deploys are as reproducible as possible.

Once you need a plug-in, you must also start to follow the pattern of using a *package.json* to manage your Node.js dependencies, even if your project is not written in Node.js. While that may not be the end of the world, it is an additional step (usually involving npm install) in your documentation and deployment.

Cloud Resources and Permissions

Managing the permissions of a cloud account is an often overlooked and misunderstood part of living in someone else's datacenters.

First, you have to understand that each resource in the cloud that can take any form of action on any part of your cloud provider other than itself requires some form of identity. If you have an API gateway that allows an HTTP request to be processed by a function, that API gateway needs an identity, and that identity needs permission to invoke that specific function.

If you're using AWS, all of your resources will have an *Amazon Resource Name* (ARN). Think of it as a URL for a resource in the cloud—not for how it is publicly found on the internet, but how it is found inside the cloud account. Following are the example formats provided by Amazon (*https://oreil.ly/LAZU-*):

```
arn:partition:service:region:account-id:resource-id
arn:partition:service:region:account-id:resource-type/resource-id
arn:partition:service:region:account-id:resource-type:resource-id
```

We will have to use these to create the permissions for our cloud systems. For most AWS systems, the partition will be `aws`. When creating rules for permissions, you can omit certain parts such as `region` or `account`, as a wildcard to make a permission as permissive as possible. The following is an example of a *role statement*, essentially a rule granting or denying permission:

```
Effect: Allow
Action:
  - s3:PutObject
Resource: "arn:aws:s3:::MySpecialBucket"
```

This statement allows an entity (in the case of your *serverless.yml* file, your functions) to put objects into a specific S3 bucket. Actions are granular, so this example does not allow you to read or list objects in that same bucket. This would mean the function could not verify the file is actually there. You can find the different actions in the AWS documentation.

For the `resource-id` component of an ARN, you can also use an asterisk (*) to create a wildcard, such as `arn:aws:s3:::Learning-Serverless-*`. This would allow that role statement to work for any buckets that we can access in our account with that naming scheme.

Having to manage and update these permissions can be a sharp edge, especially when first learning how to manage infrastructure in the cloud. The more granular the permissions, the better regarded they are. However, nobody, especially not those who are used to wielding `sudo` permissions, enjoys red "access denied" error messages. One way to simplify things is by using namespacing. For example, it is unlikely that your service should have access to all DynamoDB tables across your account, but it makes sense for your service to have access to all of *its* DynamoDB tables. By prefixing your resources with the name of the service, and the stage, you can be more generous with your permissions, while maintaining granularity and good security posture.

Similarly, while the role deploying your service might need the ability to create DynamoDB tables, it should not be able to read or write from them. You may choose to safeguard your tables further by disallowing anyone from deleting them. As such, permissions are a major part of the architecture of your cloud application.

If you are not the owner of the cloud provider account you are using, you may run into permissions errors while creating, managing, and deploying your serverless systems. If available, use a sandbox AWS account, or one where you can control permissions to craft the correct permissions, or else you will find yourself brute forcing them.

Infrastructure Templates

When using the Serverless Framework with AWS, Google Cloud, or Azure, the components of your service described by your *serverless.yml* file will be adapted into the native infrastructure templating format of your cloud provider. For AWS that is CloudFormation; for Google, Deployment Manager; and for Azure, Resource Manager.

If your team is already using other tools to manage infrastructure, you can create a deployment package using the Serverless Framework that may be deployable using the other tools. For example, you can deploy a CloudFormation template using a tool such as Terraform.

Production Secrets

Your production secrets, such as a password to connect to a database or an API token for a third-party service, should never be kept in your Git repository unencrypted. The best practice is to use a secrets store, which may create issues with bursts of traffic across your lambdas, or to utilize something like the AWS Key Management Service to encrypt these secrets. Then in the initialization code for your functions, they will need to decrypt these secrets.

.gitignore

It *is* expected that you are familiar with using Git, a popular form of version control. Many people who use Git don't really know it well, but for the purpose of this chapter I want to make sure you are familiar with the *.gitignore* file.

The *.gitignore* file lives in the root of a Git repository and must be checked into that repository in order to take effect. It lists files and file patterns that tell Git to exclude files and paths from being considered as files of the repository. This is not foolproof as it does not affect files currently in the repository or added manually with an override. You may want to use Git *hooks*, a method of running scripts at certain parts of the Git life cycle, such as when committing code, to ensure that files with secrets are kept out of the repository. Once there, they live on forever by default, as that is the point of version control. The only way to remove them is to find the correct incantation of `git filter-branch` to run in order to remove them from every single commit in the repository.

If you utilize a method that allows you to have a local unencrypted version of these secrets for testing and development (hopefully nonproduction secrets, but secrets nonetheless), stored in a file, make sure to include that filename or pattern in the *.gitignore* file of your project. Secrets are no longer secret once they are in your Git repository. If you are using a method where they are stored in an encrypted form, it is acceptable to store them in your repository, although the practices of your organization may dictate otherwise.

The Components of a serverless.yml File

The *serverless.yml* file is where the Serverless Framework expects to find the configuration that is required to deploy your application code to its intended target. This file is how you define the infrastructure of your service. The file can contain multiple functions, the events that trigger them, and the other resources that comprise the service. It will also be the home to enabling plug-ins and their configuration.

There should be one *serverless.yml* per service, and each service should be independently deployed. In a microservices architecture, each microservice will have its own *serverless.yml* file.

At its root, the *serverless.yml* file is the root of a dictionary, or a key value mapping. I will cover each part of the file as its own section, but realize that you can have a valid configuration without including every section. I will talk about the basics of what goes into each section, then I will show you how this works in practice with examples of adding infrastructure that requires changes in multiple sections.

Provider

This is where you define and configure the cloud provider you will rely on for your service (see Example 5-3). If your service is meant to be deployed to multiple cloud providers, you may want to rely on multiple *serverless.yml* files, as configuring this in one file may be daunting and confusing, and the results may be brittle.

Example 5-3. Provider section of serverless.yml

```
provider:
  name: learning-serverless
  runtime: python3.8
  stage: dev
  region: us-east-1
  iamRoleStatements:
    Effect: Allow
    Action:
      - s3:GetObject
      - s3:PutObject
    Resource: "arn:aws:s3:::Learning-Serverless-*"
```

This is also where you define the `runtime` that will execute your code, as well as the region for your infrastructure. Many of these settings are overridable in the relevant sections.

The *stage* allows you to have multiple versions of the service running, such as dev, staging, and production. The stage will get incorporated into the names of all of the functions, but you must make sure to incorporate it into the names of any other resources being created. Also make sure to consider the stage as part of the resource name for your cloud permissions. Lastly, it is a best practice to separate your production and nonproduction services into different accounts or projects with your cloud provider. Using the same account for both can lead to taking down a vital system, or even worse, complete loss of data. A development account should be safe and permissive to allow developers to understand what is possible without taking down the company. A QA account should have as much parity as possible with Production, without using any of the same secrets or data. Lastly, the Production account should be as locked down as possible. One system failing as a result of too restrictive permissions is better than all systems failing due to overly permissive permissions.

Also, if you are deploying to multiple regions, you can configure which *region* to use through the serverless tool; keep in mind that you will have to run the deploy command multiple times, one for each region. You will also have to be mindful of failures in this deployment process and roll back if one region is successful and another is not. You can override the role specified in the file using a command-line argument on the serverless tool, -r.

For AWS, you will also configure the *permissions* of the role used by your collections of lambdas here. If you are not able to make changes to the permissions on your cloud account, you can instead specify a role in this section, and have your cloud team grant the permissions you would like to that role. This is generally safer in a large organization, as you want to minimize the number of people able to control such things.

On AWS, this is also where you will add any required *tags* for your infrastructure for other tools in your organizations workflow. These tags may be used to define the owner, or route an alert to the proper people in the event of an incident. They may also be used to break down the costs of the infrastructure.

If you do not have the ability to manage your own permissions, I will share a shortcut with you: you can add a value for the role, under this section, with the *ARN* for the role your operations teams have created for your service's functions. You can keep the `iamRoleStatements` section, but comment it out. When the needs for your permissions change, you can comment out the role, and uncomment the `iamRoleStatements`. You can then create a deployment package (covered in "Deployment" on page 80), and share the CloudFormation template, or the extracted permissions from that template, with your operations teams so they can update the role. Finally, uncomment the role and recomment the `iamRoleStatements`.

Environment

This is where you store environment variables for all of the functions inside of each service (see Example 5-4). Each function can also have additional environment variables specific to it, but that would go under the next section.

Example 5-4. Environment section of serverless.yml

```
environment:
  MEDIA_BUCKET: Learning-Serverless-Media
```

You may store the names of resources or other configurable options here. I like to think of this as what levers you are exposing to an operator of the system. Because each function can have its own value, you can have simple environment variables such as one I call `CLOSING_TIME`. When I have a function that will try to do as much work as possible in a given invocation, it needs to keep track of how much time is remaining, and cleanly exit so as not to incur a retry. For that, I would set the variable with the amount of time, in seconds, the function would like allocated for closing up shop. Instead of having multiple `CLOSING_TIME` variables per function or task, you can keep the simple name, and set it with a default value for the whole service as well as different values, as needed.

You may need to store secrets for your service to run correctly. As previously mentioned, do not put such secrets directly into your *serverless.yml* file, unencrypted.

Functions

This section is where you define your functions and the events that will trigger them, as in Example 5-5.

Example 5-5. Functions section of serverless.yml

```
functions:
  hello:
    handler: functions.hello_function
    events:
      - http:
          path: users/create
          method: get
  periodic-task-example:
    handler: functions.periodic_task_example
    events:
      - schedule: rate(10 minutes)
```

Defining certain events will automatically create and configure the underlying infrastructure. Other event definitions will require existing resources. Some events will create the infrastructure for you if you omit the details, or rely on your configuration if you add the additional configuration, such as specifying an *ARN*. Different types of events will require different types of infrastructure and configuration, and it is best to read the documentation for the specific event type. The documentation for the Serverless Framework includes a section for each event, and any events added by plug-ins should have adequate documentation as well.

There are many options for the events that can invoke a function, depending on the destination for your service. The best source is the documentation for each cloud provider. Additional event sources can be installed via plug-in as well.

Resources

This section is only used for AWS (at least currently). In this section, you will define the additional components or resources of your service (see Example 5-6). This syntax is taken directly from CloudFormation, and the AWS docs are the best resource for finding all of the available options.

Example 5-6. Resources section of serverless.yml

```
resources:
  Resources:
    MediaBucket:
      Type: AWS::S3::Bucket
      Properties:
        BucketName: Learning-Serverless-Media
```

Package

This is where you configure what files should, and shouldn't be, included in the bundle or your application code that will be created and deployed to the cloud (see Example 5-7).

Example 5-7. Package section of serverless.yml

```
package:
  include:
    - config/**
    - include-me.py
    - include-me-dir/**
  exclude:
    - config/production-secrets
    - exclude-me.py
    - exclude-me-dir/**
```

Make sure to include the code or packaged build of the code, and make sure to exclude any unnecessary files or any sensitive files, such as the credentials or environment variable files, if you are doing things in that way.

You will need to include the dependencies of your project. If any of your dependencies are compiled (and they might be, even if the language you are using isn't compiled), you will need to make sure to build them for the correct OS running in your cloud provider's function environment. For example, the plug-in `serverless-python-requirements` uses a Docker container to take care of building the requirements of your Python project so that they will run.

Depending on the needs of your project or organization, you might not use the Serverless Framework for deploying, but that doesn't mean you can't use it for packaging up your code to be deployed. We will cover this later in Chapter 8.

Plug-Ins

Plug-ins extend the functionality of the Serverless Framework. The plug-in engine is very powerful, and there are some amazing plug-ins already made. Some plug-ins are official and hosted on the serverless organization on GitHub. Others can be found on their website, or the NPM repository. You can also make your own (which you can publish internally, externally, or not at all). Regardless of source, this is where you enable them (see Example 5-8).

Example 5-8. Example of the plug-ins section of serverless.yml

```
plugins:
  - serverless-offline
```

When relying on a plug-in—or any other software that you did not develop—for your production systems, you are still responsible for the code contained within. You must do some due diligence to make sure that it is not only safe, but that the implementation will work for you. For example, your organization may have standards that are not followed by the plug-in, or even the Serverless Framework itself.

The following are some examples of plug-ins:

`serverless-graphql`
An example of a plug-in that enables an integration with a newer managed service before it makes its way into official Serverless Framework support.

`serverless-offline`
Allows you to run local versions of functions for local development.

`serverless-python-requirements`

An almost essential plug-in if you are using Python. This builds your *requirements.txt* file inside a Docker container that resembles the AWS Lambda environment so you don't have to.

`serverless-scriptable-plugin`

This can help you add other parts to your deployment and tooling without having to write JavaScript. This could be how you build other components, such as static files if they are part of your service as well.

Custom

This is where you can store extra variables for reference in other parts of your configuration, or where a plug-in might allow you to override a default setting (see Example 5-9).

Example 5-9. Custom section of serverless.yml

```
custom:
  stuff: It's what you want.
  you_can_put:
    - anything
    - you
    - want
  to:
    reference: elsewhere
    in: this file
```

Namespacing for Sanity and Security

In addition to clarity of ownership when an administrator is viewing the cloud dashboard, this namespacing is important for security and helps to define the blast radius, a concept we discussed in Chapter 3.

Serverless already provides some amount of namespacing when using its default built-in functionality, but you may have to configure this if it is incompatible with your organization's standards or existing resources. You may also have to keep the namespacing performed by the Serverless Framework in mind when creating your own resources or defining them manually or with plug-ins. Remember, consistency is key in keeping things clear and well organized in the dashboard of your cloud provider.

If you share your cloud account with any other services, you will want to be thoughtful about namespacing your resources, as they are entities in their own right. Depending on the size of your organization, it may make sense to have multiple accounts. Your organization can still have one bill, and one set of common rules applied against all subaccounts, so this may be helpful for also avoiding issues when teams share service limits.

Using the serverless Command

The command-line tool is your main interface to operate the Serverless Framework. It has a set of commands built in, and some plug-ins for additional functionality. Through the following steps and examples, we will cover the most commonly used commands of the Serverless Framework.

For these steps, we are going to rely heavily on the documentation and sample projects available on *https://www.serverless.com*. By doing this, I can cover multiple cloud providers and multiple languages. I will walk you through the overall steps in deploying a sample project, and during each step you can pause and follow along the linked detailed instructions provided by the project. After we deploy the sample project of your choosing, I will get into the details of how you will build on the examples provided to meet the needs of your applications.

Installing Serverless

To get started, you will install the Serverless Framework using the Node.js package manager:

1. Install Node.js using a package manager (*https://oreil.ly/5bD3G*) or an installer (*https://oreil.ly/cJVqE*).

2. Install the Serverless Framework by running `npm install -g serverless` in your terminal.

You may subsequently choose to turn off the *telemetry*, or usage data sharing, by running `serverless slstats --disable` in your terminal.[2] While it may be helpful to provide usage data to the creators of a tool, you, or your organization, may not be comfortable with sharing data from such a sensitive environment. Your organization may also consider blocking all outside internet access in your build pipeline, and only allowing certain URL patterns through.

---

2 Telemetry can either be voting or surveillance, depending on your personal ideology. You can read more about `slstats` at *https://oreil.ly/XnjYf*.

Setting Up Serverless with Credentials

We will rely on the documentation from the Serverless Framework to get set up with our cloud provider:

- Amazon Web Services (*https://oreil.ly/lnoso*)
- Google Cloud (*https://oreil.ly/gwMwI*)
- Microsoft Azure (*https://oreil.ly/6lXxR*)

There are a couple of key takeaways, at least from the AWS version of these instructions:

Tokens
> To access your cloud provider programmatically, you will rely on tokens. You can generally generate them yourself per the instructions, but your organization may have that functionality restricted. In that case, rely on your organization's method for getting tokens, and setting them up for AWS tooling on your command line.

Permission
> For your deployment, or some of the other commands like invoke, to work locally, you will need permission. Depending on your use case, you may not want developers to have access to invoke production lambdas directly.

Pulling in Templates Using serverless install

You can either use `serverless install` to start with a sample project, or use `serverless create` in a new or existing repository to create the basic scaffolding needed.

If your project requires the use of plug-ins, you will need to install these dependencies using the Node.js package manager, or `npm`. Here's how:

1. Go to the examples page (*https://oreil.ly/D7ozp*).
2. Find the "Simple HTTP Endpoint" example project for your preferred cloud provider and vendor if it exists, or you can, follow along on this Serverless.com page (*https://oreil.ly/BKG1x*).
3. The following command will create a folder with the example project, so you may first wish to navigate to your preferred directory for such projects. (If you are using a different example project, you will find the equivalent command there.) In your terminal, run the following: `serverless install -u https://github.com/serverless/examples/tree/master/aws-python-simple-http-endpoint -n aws-python-simple-http-endpoint`.
4. Navigate, or `cd` into the newly created folder, *aws-python-simple-http-endpoint* or the name of the example you have chosen.

Inspecting the Package of Our Sample Project (What's Inside)

In computer security, there is a concept known as "trust, but verify." Sometimes you or your organization have to trust something, such as an open source library, but that does not mean you have to do it blindly. If you or your organization audit the code on GitHub for a library, or even for your programming language, you still take a leap of faith by assuming that a pip or npm install will get the same code onto your computer, or even worse, your servers. But that is part of the trust your organization has to have with GitHub as it may also host your company's software code, and could hack you even more directly and surgically. Your option here is not to trust GitHub at all, and for most, that's just not practical. You have to trust even more than that to jump to the conclusion that it is safe to run, but for the purposes of practical paranoia, you can learn when to trust but verify. You trust the NPM community to deliver safe code, else you wouldn't use it. But you need to verify that, as others have found out the hard way, compromised packages exist. Maybe, the hackers were just after free mining power, but sometimes they're after more than that.

It makes sense to verify these files. Take a look at what we are going to send to the cloud. Start by looking at the *README* file. Then, look at the *serverless.yml* file, and finally the application code. You don't need to perform a code review, and may not have the requisite experience at this point, but you should be able to identify that there are no security red flags.

Deployment

To deploy this project, simply run serverless deploy. Sit back and watch the terminal output. Upon success, it should display the created resources, including the HTTP endpoint for your first function.

Cash Rules Everything Around Me

Before we deploy, we should quickly mention the costs incurred with your cloud provider. All of the supporting services from your cloud provider may have cost implications.

Not everything we are doing here may be under the free tier. Instructions for how to destroy a provisioned service are provided later so you can remove these test projects to avoid incurring additional costs.

Invoking the Function, and Viewing Logs

If you want to manually test your function you can invoke it using the `serverless` command:

1. Run `serverless invoke -f currentTime` to see the current time.
2. Note the URL for the endpoint created when you deployed. If you have lost it, you can run `serverless info` to output information about the service, including the endpoint.
3. Run `serverless log -f currentTime -t` to *tail*, or follow, the logs of the function.
4. In a separate terminal, `curl` the endpoint URL, or access it in a browser.

You should see the logging information in near-real time.

Rollbacks

The Serverless Framework command-line tool also allows for an easy rollback in the case of a bad deployment. By default, the framework keeps the last five deployments (the CloudFormation template, as well as the application code), so that you can easily roll back with one line. It is important to note that some organizations will have a policy of *rolling forward*: creating and deploying a new version instead of going backwards to a previously known working one.

Because we have only performed one deploy, there is nothing to roll back *to*; however, you can use `serverless deploy list` to see the deployed versions, and `serverless rollback` to perform a roll back if needed. I would recommend experimenting with this before you need it in order to better understand its operation.

Destroying the Service

To avoid any additional costs, start by doing the following:

```
serverless remove
```

Any steps you may have manually followed to make changes to your cloud provider account to set up an additional service may have to be deprovisioned manually as well. One example, would be remove the IAM policies or the IAM users you have created if they are no longer needed. But doing that can have consequences if they are being relied on somehow, such as if you are still using those permissions to deploy and manage other services in the same account.

Be mindful of any errors when running this command, and verify by accessing your dashboard that all of these resources have been destroyed.

Deployment Packages

In many organizations, you will not be able to deploy in this manner for generally valid reasons dictated from above. No worries. Instead, you can utilize `serverless package` to create a deployment package. The deployment package will be a Cloud-Formation template and a `.zip` file of your application code and requirements. You can then follow your organization's procedures with actions such as making a pull request with your CloudFormation template, or shipping the `.zip` file to an artifact management system for further validation and deployment. If these actions require separate steps, make sure the `.zip` file first gets uploaded to an appropriate S3 bucket before the CloudFormation template (which points your functions to that specific uploaded file) gets deployed.

Real-World serverless.yml

It is doubtful that your service will consist of only functions. There are many ins and outs of expanding your service with the *serverless.yml* file. To walk you through the basics, here is a specific example of adding a managed database to our service.

We are going to use DynamoDB to illustrate the additional configuration you will need to add a managed service with your cloud provider. You will need to consider other things such as the permissions of your function to access the resources you have created, and also the permissions of the user account that will deploy the resource initially, and even the permissions to later modify it. (We will discuss this type of permissioning later in Chapter 9.)

If you are going to follow along for the next steps, you should be working from this GitHub site (*https://oreil.ly/kyW-3*). You do not need to follow these steps now, but later when you are adding different resources to create your architecture, they will be here as a reference.

Let's talk about what is different in this example from the hello world one that we deployed. At the end of the *serverless.yml* file, you will see the following has been added:

```
resources:
  Resources:
    NicknamesTable:
      Type: 'AWS::DynamoDB::Table'
      Properties:
        AttributeDefinitions:
          - AttributeName: firstName
            AttributeType: S
        KeySchema:
          - AttributeName: firstName
            KeyType: HASH
        ProvisionedThroughput:
```

```
        ReadCapacityUnits: 1
        WriteCapacityUnits: 1
        TableName: ${self:provider.environment.DYNAMODB_TABLE}
```

Setting Environment Variables

As previously mentioned, the resources section is where you put additional resources using the CloudFormation syntax. The preceding block describes a DynamoDB table that will be created. From the name, you can see that there is some form of templating being used. The Serverless Framework has templating built in for your configurations so you can keep the variables of your project tidy, and adopt your files to the different stages and regions they may be deployed to. The preceding example reads from `self`, which is the *serverless.yml* file, and then reads the DYNAMODB_TABLE value from the environment variables set in the provider section:

```
provider:
  # This is toward the beginning of the provider section
  environment:
    DYNAMODB_TABLE: ${self:service}-${self:provider.stage}
```

This is where that value is set. Here it is exposed to the functions that will run in this service. This example itself, is using variables to create the value, although it would be best if there were a name appended to this, such as `${self:service}-${self:provider.stage}-nicknames`.

Modify Permissions

Under the provider section of the *serverless.yml* file, you will see the following has been added to allow for the functions of this service to have access to the database we have created. This may be different from how you normally connect to a database. Traditionally, you may have used a connection string, or a combination of IP address and port, with a username and password. When connecting to a managed database such as DynamoDB, you may have to connect using the cloud provider's API, which is authenticated through something such as IAM. When connecting to other hosted databases such as PostgreSQL or MySQL, you will still use the connection string style method, but you will have to ensure that your lambdas have access to the VPC with your database:

```
provider:
  # This is at the end of the provider section
  iamRoleStatements:
    - Effect: Allow
      Action:
        - dynamodb:GetItem
        - dynamodb:UpdateItem
      Resource: >
        arn:aws:dynamodb:${opt:region,
        self:provider.region}:*:table/${self:provider.environment.DYNAMODB_TABLE}
```

Conclusion

There are many moving parts to creating, configuring, deploying, and managing your cloud infrastructure, but you are now familiar with the basics. The Serverless Framework aims to simplify these responsibilities, but don't get caught up in copying too much from others, as every use case is different. At the end of the day, you are responsible for every line of code you push into production—even the lines you did not write. Configuration for your cloud provider can be more powerful and dangerous than your application code, so you need to fully understand the documentation from your cloud provider, the requirements of your organization, and the evolving best practices of the community.

CHAPTER 6

Monitoring, Observability, and Alerting

This job would be great if it weren't for the customers.
—Randal Graves, *Clerks*

What Is Monitoring?

Once you have your service in the cloud, it begins to take on a whole new life. That lovely deterministic behavior you have witnessed while developing and testing your code is long gone. Your service has now been sent out to face the internet, and with that traffic comes unexpected states of entities in your systems. Bugs start to surface, and these perfectly chaotic flows of user actions and their consequences will likely cause some form of degraded service in your system at least once, if not total failure and lack of availability. When this happens, how are you supposed to know that your service is even down in the first place?

Monitoring.

Monitoring is the component of your application that enables you to detect incidents and understand why they are occurring in order to attempt to fix them. It is the way to confirm when things have returned to normal. It is how you interrogate the health and status of your systems.

But monitoring is much more than that. It is your best tool to avoid failure in the first place. With monitoring, you expose the health of your application and all of its services in real time so that you can detect anomalies before they snowball into incidents. Emitting the right metrics and being able to understand and interpret them are skills that everyone on your team must learn. In modern engineering organizations, developers no longer just toss their code over the proverbial fence and leave the consequences to the system administrators. Instead, developers now own, or share, this responsibility.

Either you have already been bitten by the monitoring bug and your life has never been the same since, or you are operating in the dark ages. In this chapter, we will cover the basic constructs of monitoring, how to assemble them into a basic monitoring system, and touch on some, but nowhere near all, advanced practices to open up your thinking and accept monitoring into your life.

Why Do We Need Monitoring?

Monitoring the health of your systems for anomalous values for key metrics and having the right people notified about the situation can be time-consuming to initially set up; however, it is critical to delivering a reliable system using automation.

Automation is a fundamental tenet of a successful DevOps culture. The simplest automation is to measure the health of your systems using monitoring to detect anomalous values for key metrics, then notifying the right people about the situation.

Another use case of monitoring is to measure something in real time as the answer to a question. Unsure of the likelihood of the edge case? Emit a metric before you implement the feature, or as the error handling for the unhappy path. Engineering is always about making trade-offs; with monitoring, you can make an informed decision. You can find out if it is worth it to prioritize implementing a new feature, handling an edge case, or just having a better understanding of how events and data flow through your services.

How does your organization define and measure success? It may use a system for goal setting known as *key performance indicators* (KPIs). If so, you can likely measure these key metrics, or other metrics that are important to the health of your systems or the business as a whole, in real time, with notifications when you reach significant milestones.

Your application or service(s) may have to abide by a *service-level agreement* (SLA), a contract that defines specific metrics your technology must meet, such as having service availability 99.9% of the time. How do you maintain such a commitment? How can you commit to staying below a certain error rate if you don't measure such things?

How Does Monitoring Relate to Serverless?

Many developers and system administrators perform a remote login to the server using a *Secure Shell* (SSH) to investigate issues with a production system. But the more distributed your system becomes, the less useful and practical such a method becomes. Not just because the environments are becoming increasingly ephemeral and disposable, but also because effective operations in such a system are stateless by nature. Even if you could SSH into a serverless function, it wouldn't help you understand the health of the overall system.

In a serverless world, you may be able to understand and plan your scaling, and then set alerts accordingly using monitoring. For example, if you have a limit on the number of concurrent invocations, you can set alarms to know when you are approaching them to avoid approaching or exceeding the limit. But what about just raising limits ahead of time? There can be cost and other issues (like pummeling other services with traffic) that make you want to keep those limits in check. A good rule of thumb is that every limit should be balanced by an alarm. Also remember that service limit changes may have a lead time and that you may hit service limits because of an anomaly that prevents legitimate work from being performed.

The On-Ramp to Automation

Getting started with monitoring as described in this chapter is the first step toward saving more time, and preventing mistakes and oversights, with an automation-first approach to DevOps.

In order to get to more automation, you need to have the right inputs for the processes you are going to automate, and that will generally come in the form of metrics. It also comes in the form of alarms. Depending on your cloud provider, you may be able to receive notification of certain events occurring in your cloud account to react to such changes automatically. You can even add a serverless function to react in scale to these events automatically to save money by throttling up and down different resources in response to user traffic or other inputs.

What Are My Options?

There are a growing number of providers in the monitoring space and many of them have unique value propositions, so make sure the tool you choose can handle the basics, and handle them well. You will want to thoroughly kick the tires, as monitoring tools can improve over time with the accumulation of historical data for metrics; but *caveat emptor*, there is no clean migration path for historical data when moving between providers. Depending on your needs, the built-in tooling from your cloud provider may be sufficient, and in the current world of serverless functions, the nature of ephemeral containers for compute may limit your options to get telemetry out reliably without incurring any additional overhead.

Relying on your cloud provider may be the easiest way to get metrics out of your systems. They might be the only way, in the case of certain metrics about the health of lower-level systems or managed services; using another tool will require shipping those metrics to the vendor.

Hosted SaaS Offerings

There may be a simple reason why the built-in monitoring metrics from your cloud provider don't feel like enough. One such example is if your organization is operating in multiple clouds.

If your organization has selected such a solution, take full advantage of the vendor lock-in: watch some of their conference presentations to learn to use that tool to its fullest advantage. But also use abstraction to stay as decoupled from the vendor as possible, in case the political winds in your organization change or you want to A/B test vendors in the future. (This pattern is covered later in the chapter.)

When designing your monitoring plans, it is best to understand the offerings, limitations, and even pricing of the vendor you are using. A developer may want to measure something they see as benign but rack up a huge bill because they don't understand how usage is measured. For example, DataDog may only charge $5 per serverless function per month, but that is an approximation for having 40 custom metrics per function. This may suffice if you split out each component of your service to individual functions, but it might not work if you ship a monolith into a single function. What's more, you could end up overpaying for this particular service if you split services into multiple functions.

Utilizing a hosted solution allows you to focus on the value you are creating for your users instead of on the infrastructure of self-hosting an open source solution, although you may still need some way to log all of the monitoring metrics if you want to truly own your monitoring data.

Self-Hosted and Open Source

Many people struggle with running their own tooling for a particular part of their applications. If you've chosen serverless, I would imagine you are not too concerned with creating, managing, and scaling a cluster of services to gain insights into your production application—there is an overwhelming array of choices out there.

You may want to avoid building your own tools at first and use SaaS solutions or the cloud provider tools. If you build your own monitoring, you have to monitor it and keep it up! But it makes sense to build tools, automation, and so forth around monitoring providers and services. If you build your own monitoring or tooling, you may want to be sure to keep it serverless if you want it to scale in the same way as your services.

Just because tool X worked for team Y does not mean it will work for you. Make sure you are solving for your problems specifically, not just adapting a popular choice. Think about what you need to know about your systems and then find the tools that do that, and change them as you need to. Sometimes, you will have to build your own tools. But remember that you must maintain those tools as well.

Before you make a decision here, consider: if you are going to have your own monitoring platform, will there be a team you can adequately staff to handle those needs, not only now but as they grow and reach new levels of scale? Someone in your organization may push a change that clobbers your monitoring system, but monitoring utilization can spike with any and every other spike in your system. When your team is already scrambling to identify and fix a failing system, losing your monitoring system will not only make it more difficult, but could prevent you from investigating the health of any system during that outage. That being said, you may work somewhere that has already made this decision and so you fall into this category, as may be the case for organizations with enhanced requirements for data storage.

Components of Monitoring

Monitoring is not a switch you can turn on and automatically have its full benefits, nor is it confined to one problem and one tool. It must include metrics and logging, and may be enhanced with *application performance monitoring* (APM) as well. I'll limit the conversation here to monitoring as it relates to collecting, aggregating, reporting, and alerting on metrics. Logging, which is the same but for statements instead of metrics, will be covered in the next chapter. Also, many providers and vendors offer an APM system. These systems offer granular data about application performance, on a per-function (the application code kind) basis, with the time consumed with all network requests, including accessing data from your datastores.

Monitoring can be a difficult concept to grasp if you are unfamiliar with it. To illustrate the application of these topic as we cover them, we are going to bring monitoring to the latest fictional streaming service, Dry+, where you can watch an extensive library of paints, lacquers, and solvents dry. Dry+ is relatively simple from the user perspective. On the web, a smartphone, or a smart TV, a user can sign up for a subscription plan, manage their existing plan, browse and search different types of materials and conditions (you know, for the drying videos), and watch and control videos.

Metrics

Effective monitoring is both an art and a science. Deciding what to measure is not something you should expect to get right on the first attempt. Just like the entire system, metrics are a dynamic thing that can change from one millisecond to the next. You need to determine what metrics best measure the health of your systems and even your organization.

What to measure

You can quickly start by coming up with metrics that support or directly measure your KPIs, such as *new user subscriptions*. Next, consider the metrics that measure your ability to drive those KPIs in real time, such as *new users on the subscription checkout page*. Finally, you can't reach any of these KPIs without a healthy service up and running, so you'll need to come up with metrics to determine the health and stress levels of your services, such as *user traffic* or *database utilization*.

That may seem like a daunting task, but it all starts with the users. What actions and sequences will users take through a system, and how can you measure those? Not for analytical reasons for marketing, although monitoring metrics can serve as a proxy for that, but as analytics for the occupants of the architecture you and possibly others have erected. Think about the criticality of these sequences. Which actions or sequences, if they fail, signal larger worries for the availability of your application? Which of these constitute an outage? If the ability for a user to "check out" a virtual shopping cart starts creating more errors than expected, how will you react? Keep in mind, too, that the root cause of your incident can be increased user traffic; be sure to measure that as well.

For example, imagine a metric that measures login attempts on the Dry+ website, mobile app, and smart TVs. You may want to augment that data with tags, such as the device type, browser type, or the country of origin of the request. If the production system is unaware of the country as it does not affect its operation, it might not be important as a component of the metric. But if it is important for something else, such as the security of the system, it might make sense to enrich the metrics by adding additional processing. In other cases, it might make sense to process other data out of band to achieve the desired metric. For example, you could use the access logs to determine login attempts from the URL, and information from the headers (such as IP address, or the locale of the user's device). Also, when considering tags, you want to consider the balance between readability of the tags and the constraints of the monitoring system. For example, "The United States of America" might be too long to be supported as a tag. It might make sense to use the ISO two-letter abbreviations instead. But that might be difficult for less technical users to understand, so you could try another method, such as custom country names. But that involves adding even more code to the application. Starting to recognize the pattern? Your application should not have to bend over backward to emit useful metrics. While you may choose to do so for logging, where details become more important, constrain the implementation of metrics coming from your application code to those that are vital, and keep away from adding complexity for metrics that are *nice to have*. If understanding a certain measure is important, you may need to add more code to craft the metric. Just make sure to write your code in a way that does not prevent the surrounding code from functioning, and add unit tests.

System metrics

System metrics are provided by your cloud provider or a monitoring agent about underlying systems (or servers). These metrics can indicate the health of a system by providing an insight into the usage of resources such as CPU, memory, network, and disk space. In the world of serverless, some of these metrics might be the number of invocations, execution durations, and throttles if your function is rate limited.

For a database, system metrics can include the number of connections and replication health, in addition to the base system metrics. (Databases can run out of space too.) If a component is a managed service, the details may not be exposed as they are not relevant to you as a consumer of the service, but I guarantee the people managing those services are keeping an eye on them.

Just because all of your infrastructure might be serverless, and you do not need to concern yourself with the underlying servers, metrics regarding these systems may still be available and of use in your overall monitoring and alerting strategy. Some of the system or provider metrics available to you will be the closest proxy you can get to the real user actions occurring outside of your system. This might be overall requests per second if you are using a content distribution network (CDN) such as CloudFront or Cloudflare. Keep in mind that the root cause of your incident can be increased user traffic, so you need to measure that as well.

If you have metrics from other vendors or services you use, you may want to utilize a SaaS metrics offering that can bring all of these disparate metrics to the same place, or a custom-built one if your organization is large enough to need and use it. Remember, these metrics will be the basic building blocks that allow us to build visual representations of the health of a system. As such, having all of the data in one place may be needed to have an easy and consistent way to understand the health of a system at a glance.

Custom metrics

Application, or custom, metrics are those metrics that you emit about your systems. There is no way for your monitoring tool to know the intimate details of your business logic and the importance of each action taken. You have to create these events by adding metrics to your code.

The two basic metrics available to add are *increments* and *gauges*. An increment (counter) is when you want each event to add to the other events occurring during the same time period. For example, if you want to keep track of the count of an action or event, such as a user login. An increment is not limited to simply being increased by 1, but can be increased by any number within the limitations of your monitoring provider. Increments can only be increased or reset. A gauge measures a value of something as an observation at a given time. During a given time period, the last gauge will indicate the reading, but for counters, the value will be a sum of all measurements in that period of time. For example, a gauge could measure a specific value in a process, while a counter keeps track of all the occurrences of that process, or the sum of the values in that process.

You'll want to keep good metrics for the entire life cycle of your services. But you won't always get them right at first. Try to capture metrics that you will want to track over long periods of time. The longer your metrics have been in place, the more historical context you have when investigating an anomalous data point or a disturbing trend appearing on the horizon of your charts. Metrics can help inform engineering decisions with basic data about trends and seasonality. Think about what kind of data you will want to be able to reflect on days, weeks, and months from now.

To avoid collisions and confusion, it's best practice to give your metrics unique names and to have clear rules about how they should be named. Effective namespacing, such as `servicename.filename.function.metric`, can avoid potential collisions. Some may choose to include the stage, such as `production`, in their metric format, but I would encourage you to include that data as a tag so that you can use the same dashboard across different environments.

Metrics can be augmented with tags that allow you to add metadata to the measurements being collected. The most common tag to add is the stage in which the observation was generated. For Dry+, you may want to include information about which plan a user has with their metrics. For example, if they are on a plan with ads, versus a plan without ads, it could have an impact in an incident, or understanding how stress on one system transfers to another, such as the ad server. Monitoring systems limit tags and have naming conventions that you should make sure to understand fully, as they can cause data to magically go missing. You can enrich events such as annotating each user sign-up with the promo code they are using, or how they were referred. This kind of information allows you to create more powerful visualizations of the data. The more your dashboards get used, the better, since it increases the awareness of how your team or organization is working to achieve their goals and meet their commitments.

Never log or emit a metric that contains personal data. It is perfectly acceptable to emit a metric tagged with the state of a user, but you shouldn't include any *personally identifiable information* (PII). Don't send customer data to your monitoring or even logging tools. Doing so can make compliance impossible, especially with strengthening laws improving consumer privacy. There may be other rules inside your organization that you should be familiar with for compliance reasons.

Bringing in data from other sources

Your custom metrics are not just limited to instrumenting your application code. You can bring other useful information to help understand the current health of your systems or business by writing custom code to collect metrics from external sources such as an API or even screen scraping, and emit them as metrics. With some monitoring options you may be able to bring in useful information from other sources with prebuilt integrations.

Monitoring vendor performance

You rely on your vendors and are likely compensating them for an often critical part of your system. So you need to keep tabs on them, too. Don't just rely on their status dashboard (although it could be a useful part of your automation and alerting to share updates from your vendors into a chat system).

Be sure to check the documentation of your monitoring tools for any explicit warnings or limits they give about how you utilize them. Understand the way they measure and bill to avoid any costly mistakes.

Charts/Graphs

Charts take your monitoring metrics to the next level by making it possible to visualize them. Why work on this task? Because viewing the charts you create will unlock a different kind of creativity when facing an impending incident in your production systems.

It may take some time to get it right; creating effective charts that tell you what you need to know about your application is more of an art than a science. This is the case at least for the custom metrics you are emitting, as well as combinations of those same custom metrics with other metrics, such as system level or those from managed services or other software packages where you don't generally modify the code (such as an open source database).

For example, you can use login metrics to start to understand the current traffic flowing through a certain user path, while also being able to contextualize that instantly with the insight of overlaying the history over certain time periods.

Additionally, changing the aggregation you are using can tell you different things. Think back to calculus class, if you took it: the current value of a metric can tell you something interesting, but the rate of change of that metric can indicate a trend that tells you something different.

You are discussing a feature idea with a colleague for Dry+. A key question comes up: how often do users visit a certain section of the account settings? When you are having an argument about how often one thing happens versus another, that is a perfect time to turn to metrics. You can add a line of code to track something, ship it to production, and start to get answers instead of guessing.

Functions allow you to permute the data being graphed in a limited set of ways, as made available by your cloud provider. Sometimes overlaying the same metric on the same graph multiple times, but applying different functions to each line, can instantly give you even more information about a key metric.

Some of the basic functions you should expect to have are sum, avg, min, and max. These functions are the building blocks to create more powerful visualizations that give you the most insight into the operation of your services and systems. Make sure you are familiar with all of the offerings of the tool you are using.

Documentation is a must for each graph that you create. Explain what the human operator is looking at and how to make sense of it. Reference or link to additional information in your runbook or operations manual (Chapter 11 discusses runbooks). And if there is a specific reason you chose certain functions to display the data that wouldn't be easily understood by someone unfamiliar with the system, add that reasoning to your documentation.

Dashboards

Creating a dashboard of effective charts can bring what was once an invisible system to life, with full visibility into all of the vital signs of health for your service or even the application as a whole.

Many dashboards have the ability to change the data displayed based on changing the value of a tag. You can reuse dashboards between the different stages of your services by utilizing this functionality.

Well-designed monitoring dashboards that are easy to understand and reflect the health of the service should allow you and others to detect anomalies and incidents. Here is where you are actually able to understand the health at a glance.

Generally, dashboards should allow you to adjust for the time period in which you would like to inspect. Keep in mind the different functions and options, such as avg or max, and how the choices made in selecting the graphs should be clearly reflected and easy to understand, even to a sleepy operator who is waking up to a dashboard they have never seen before.

There is no one dashboard that will solve everything for everyone. You might combine multiple tools and sources into a dashboard. Either way, you'll need a consistent set of rules and standard for all of the "official" service dashboards. Keep in mind that you can make personal dashboards for unique views of the health and performance of a service.

Important events such as deploys should be indicated on the graphs. This can help a human operator determine if an issue was directly caused by a deploy and investigate further.

Alerts/Alarms

Why sit around and watch your metrics all day when you can set an alarm? Setting an alarm is how you can have your system tell you when it is broken. If a customer tells you that your site is down or a feature is not working, it may already be too late. There will be others who experience an issue and now think less of your system, even if they didn't have the time to complain about it. Incidents should really be detected by alarms, not by humans.

Anything that can lead to an outage or degrade service in a meaningful way needs an alarm. Set an alarm for any information that you would share with a coworker immediately and directly—and would then tell your boss if you couldn't reach your coworker.

Most tools offer the ability to set two distinct levels, which we refer to generically as warning and alert, although your tool may refer to them another way. Broadly speaking, when a metric is inside the warning range, it should politely attract the attention of a human operator, but may not require any specific action other than additional observation. It may instead be used to communicate a broader situational awareness rather than an impending incident. An alert, on the other hand, occurs with a specific event and often needs immediate attention. But how can you tell the difference? You can't! At least not without adequate documentation, which most tools allow you to include with your alarms. Let people know whether they should respond to a warning as an incident or treat it as an indicator of the general health of a service. Set clear definitions of what each of these terms mean to the humans involved.

At the alert level, an alarm must be useful *and* actionable. The parameters need to be high enough to avoid noise but low enough to catch potential disruption. This may take trial and error to get right, and that beta badge of honor might make sense to include in the messaging for your early alarms. This will be one of those topics where you and the organization might need to "disagree but commit" to the agreed upon definitions and standards. Finding the correct settings for your alarms may seem like a guessing game, but you can utilize performance or *load testing* to test and calibrate your alerting thresholds, as well as to better understand how your systems function with load.

Email is not a good medium for alerts. Engineers can and will create filters to divert machine-created emails that flow in ad nauseam. Information alerts are best sent to relevant topics on the company chat system, and alarms that need to get an acknowledgment should be handled by an on-call management system such as PagerDuty.

If there is no plan of action for response, the alarm's usefulness is drastically diminished. When responding to an alert, you must have adequate documentation, ideally provided in the messaging of the alert or in the monitoring panel of the alert. In addition to providing context in the text that gets delivered with an alert, these plans should be kept in a *runbook*.

Keep a log when responding to an incident. During the heat of the moment, it can be easy to lose or misremember important pieces of data or other evidence that could help you properly understand the root cause to solve the issue. Even if it's messy, any log during your reaction is better than nothing. That log should be used to create a *root cause analysis* or a report that should contain, at minimum, the main cause of the incident, what was impacted and how, what steps were taken to restore service, and a timeline of events. The timeline should include when service degraded initially or further, when new things were learned, when actions were performed to restore service, and progress toward the restoration of service.

Additionally, make sure to utilize rich integrations with your organization's chat system. Like or it not, the new wave of chat platforms such as Slack and Mattermost have taken root in organizations of all sizes; for many, this may be an integral component of your overall monitoring and alerting strategy. Many vendors offer a solution to provide rich information about an alert to such platforms. With some of these integrations you can see a static graph associated with the alert and potentially take action, such as acknowledging or resolving an alert.

A Selection of Advanced Practices

Simply creating, maintaining, and updating the monitoring components that you are now familiar with may be all you need to have effective monitoring for your application. But there are some best practices you should be familiar with, both for their positive impact on your sanity and to understand how to build more complex and useful constructs and solutions using these components.

Heartbeats

A heartbeat is an event, generally synthetic, to determine or inquire about the health of a system. You may be familiar with creating a heartbeat or health endpoint for an application or service so that a load balancer can keep track of what nodes or servers are healthy, ready, and available to serve traffic. In the context of monitoring, we want to ensure that a heartbeat is emitted and tracked for every action of a system so we can understand that pulse in depth across the entire system. We are not concerned with the health of individual nodes; in serverless, nodes are as ephemeral as can be, and we don't manage them.

Creating synthetic heartbeats

Sometimes you can't rely on the real world to provide you with the chaos or even basic entropy for your system to be alive enough to measure. Sure, as a metric it may be fine to see zero requests coming through, but how can you know that the system is available if there are no successful executions of the most common functions? That may not be the only way to measure your system, but consider the case of an early-stage ecommerce company. It may see only a couple of checkouts a day, but each one is of great importance to the fledgling startup. A deploy of a new version may go hours without even seeing a visitor, let alone a buyer. So how do you know that your website is functioning in case you suddenly get visitors? Create a fake end-to-end test that runs against your real production system. One example would be creating an account, adding items to the cart, checking out, logging in, cancelling the purchase, and logging out. If you were to have this run via a periodic invocation every hour and report its attempt, each successful stage, and its success as metrics, you can have an alarm go off when this process no longer works. This will let you know not only if your services are down, but your dependencies as well. This *testing in production* pattern is useful when you do not have a constant flow of traffic bombarding your service, which may even be the reason you chose serverless in the first place. In this example, you may have to use a real credit card to test, and you will want to call and let the credit card company know why a mysterious charge is happening every hour from the same merchant.

Smoke Testing and/or Canaries

After you deploy, you'll want to verify that everything is working by performing a *smoke test*. A smoke test is where you test a newly deployed system by running some basic actions that are vital to the functionality of the system, in order to see if it *smells* or does not seem to be working. The idea is that as a final test of quality, the new version is testing in production for the most basic functionality—in the same spirit as plugging in a repaired kitchen appliance to make sure it doesn't catch fire.

Smoke testing has evolved into *canary* deployments, which is when you roll out a new release of your service slowly to an increasing percentage of live production traffic while measuring the health of the application using metrics. If the metrics do not appear to be healthy or appear to be a step backward in some way, the release gets cancelled, preventing a potential incident. But if the key metrics appear to be nominal, the release will be promoted to handle all traffic.

It is helpful to use metrics to ensure that new changes deployed to production are not causing a regression or worse, a complete failure of a system.

The Most Important Metric in the World

AWS Lambda offers the ability to fail an asynchronous function invocation, or an "event," into a failure queue. They label this the *dead letter queue* (DLQ). This functionality is a big game changer in the serverless world. Located on the monitoring tab of a function in the AWS console is a metric labeled "DeadLetterErrors"—the most important metric in the world (Figure 6-1).

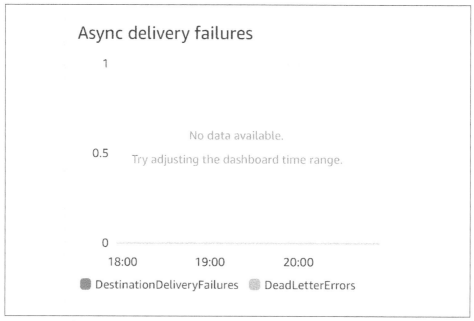

Figure 6-1. The most important metric in the world

What are "DeadLetterErrors"? They are not the number of failures that wound up in a failure queue. They are the number of failures that *failed* to get into a failure queue. Meditate on that for a second, and you may learn everything you need to know about production systems and you can throw out this book (to a friend).

When would something show up on this chart? That is a great question, especially because if it shows up here, it is gone forever. The pixel(s) on the pane are the final resting place of that job.

The two most likely cases are cloud permissions and service limits. What? You don't remember reading about dead letter queue (DLQ) limits on the AWS Lambda service limits? You must look elsewhere to find it. A DLQ is really a *Simple Queueing Service* (SQS) queue. That's not a secret: its resource identifier suggests this, and the resource lives in the SQS dashboard, not in Lambda. But SQS has service limits and you may have gone over them. As for the cloud permissions, your Lambda's execution role has permission to take the necessary actions against the SQS queue. Oh yeah, and your deploy role or someone else had the permission to make the queue in the first place. If any of these occur, your *failures* that are supposed to end up in the *failure queue* end up as a data point on this metric.

This one pane tells you everything you need to know about monitoring. Make sure important and terminal errors show up somewhere. Set an alarm on it.

Avoiding Vendor Lock-In

Regardless of the choice you make for your monitoring, whether choosing self-hosted, your cloud provider, or another vendor, your needs or preferences may change over time.

As you now are familiar, most statements to emit a metric are very simple one-liners. But what happens when you want to make a change? You will have to go and update each and every single line. While that may seem like a minor task in your text editor or *integrated development environment* (IDE) of choice, if the syntax varies too greatly, it may not be possible at all.

So my recommendation is this: no matter how simple, fast, or easy the promises being made by your monitoring tool, wrap it in a simple abstraction. This abstraction may be simple enough to only be a simple function definition in your code for each method available, with only one line of code inside.

In addition to providing a method against vendor lock-in, you can provide additional functionality (such as namespacing) to help keep your code tidy.

This method also allows you to use more than one vendor if you want to evaluate other options, or if different tools meet different needs for your organization.

This method is not just applicable for monitoring, but also for almost every third-party vendor. First, you will make it drastically easier to change in the future if your needs change, or your vendor changes or decides to shut down. Second, you can enhance your integration of third-party vendors with metrics!

If you are utilizing a vendor that is widely known by the community to have a stable and straightforward API, one that is exactly how you would have designed your abstraction around it, it may not be worth the additional time to create such an abstraction. But keep in mind in the future, if you choose to replace them, you may have to create an abstraction around the new vendor you choose, or create an internal replacement with exactly the same API.

You can test an edge case before making a feature to get a better understanding of the traffic that will flow through the service. If you are confident that the edge case would affect no or very few users, you can emit a metric and raise/return an error as a temporary placeholder for handling the edge case.

Cleaning Up Metrics and Alerts over Time

It is unlikely that you will achieve perfection on your first attempt at creating metrics and alerts. Invest time getting familiar with your tools, investigating behaviors, and testing out your monitoring. This will make it easier to use them during an incident and continuously refine them over time.

Make sure to delete temporary monitoring that is no longer useful and causes noise or costs money. But don't spend more time than it is worth—developer time might be more expensive and scarce.

If something can be simply and safely resolved, you may want to consider automation. Be mindful not to cause other issues when doing this.

Conclusion

Monitoring holds the flashlight when you're inspecting your production systems.

Monitoring takes time and effort to get right, but without them, you're flying in fog. When you have an incident, how do you know what subsystem to investigate? With monitoring, you can find your root cause more quickly and more accurately, with the evidence needed to support your findings in a proper postmortem.

Monitoring can seem intimidating and out of reach, but remember the basics. Measure and instrument vital parts of your application or service so that you better understand how they work in the real world.

CHAPTER 7

Logging

As developers, we have to communicate on many levels. We spend hours in meetings, listening and talking. We work with end users, trying to understand their needs. We write code, which communicates our intentions to a machine and documents our thinking for future generations of developers. We write proposals and memos requesting and justifying resources, reporting our status, and suggesting new approaches. And we work daily within our teams to advocate our ideas, modify existing practices, and suggest new ones. A large part of our day is spent communicating, so we need to do it well.

—David Thomas and Andrew Hunt, *The Pragmatic Programmer* (Addison-Wesley)

It is well understood that communication is fundamental to success. We can instill the value of communication into our code by infusing it with the power of logging. The story of a system in production is not written by the developer, it's written by the system—and the only way to hear that story is with logs.

Computing environments are becoming increasingly ephemeral, and interacting with an instance of your code in production may be impractical, impossible, or even illegal. Bugs in production will be an issue inside either your code or the environment it operates in. Logging can help you quickly understand how an undesired result was achieved by allowing you to manually step through the code without a debugger. It can also help increase confidence that an issue does not directly result from your code and may enable you to share that reasoning with others in a larger group effort to find the root cause. Keep in mind that not every issue (defect) that a user of your application faces will result in an incident (reduced service availability).

You will encounter issues that started as the result of a frustrated customer reaching out for support. Even if you could SSH into some machine to reproduce the user's issue, it is unlikely that the state of the system, or even that user's account, is the same, but you will have to understand what happened, when, and why in order to solve their issue. Oh yeah, and they are the lead investor of your startup. Logging will help you resolve the issue.

When you have an issue in production, your immediate reaction might be to connect to a misbehaving server and start poking around. That is not always an option, and unless you are an infrastructure or operations engineer, it is likely a bad habit. A live production server that your users are depending on that is failing does not need additional stress and entropy caused by a curious developer. And if your software runs on a client device, you can't always SSH into someone else's computer, or start up a remote desktop session and borrow their mouse while you figure out what is wrong.

Instead, you must rely on monitoring and logs. Logs provide detailed information to help you understand what has happened, find the issue, or at least reproduce it. Logs are by and for developers, just as tests are, and some developers think their lives would be better without either. But that is because they have not had the opportunity to experience the utility of these important components done correctly.

Logs allow you to extract and collect useful information about the operation of your code in the real world. And as you have learned, your local development setup is just as far away from the real world as possible.

What Does It Mean to Log?

Logging is exactly what it sounds like: keeping a log of events that have transpired or information that may be of note. It is record-keeping for your systems. But with one major caveat: logs are intended to be lossy or disposable. In fact, if you work in a regulated environment, your organization may have strict rules about when logs need to be deleted.

Data that is truly important should not be kept solely in logs. Despite the usefulness of log statements, they are not guaranteed to be delivered.[1] Nor are logs a full representation of the work being done by a system. Logs *must* be unreliable to avoid unnecessarily coupling noncritical information with critical execution of tasks. Delivering logs is a secondary function of the servers or containers running your application code. Logs are a gift, not a given.

For serverless, your logs will likely be sent first to the tooling of your cloud provider. You can set up functions to react to log statements from your other functions, or even other systems, to process the log statements and/or even send them to another log system for safekeeping.

---

1 The same goes for monitoring metrics.

Why Log?

I will give you an overview of logging before diving into the main topic of relevance, logging for your application code. Then I will talk about the logging that is available to you from the various cloud services that you use. You will likely need to enable these features if you need to have any form of auditing for compliance or regulatory reasons.

When I teach about programming, I mention "the future you." When a computer reads a piece of code, it will always read it the same (when the versions of everything have been frozen). But tomorrow, when you read code that you wrote today, it might mean something entirely different. Now imagine six months or a year from now. In addition to writing legible code and utilizing comments and/or documentation, logging can help ensure that the future you (and others) can understand a piece of code when you need to most. During a failure, effective logging allows you to leave breadcrumbs of important information that may be needed to understand the operation of code in the real world. In addition, logging can help you analyze the data of how systems work. (Although, as platforms evolve, this responsibility has shifted to monitoring for many organizations.) Your monitoring system may be able to ingest your logs, or you may be able to make a simple function that filters relevant statements into monitoring metrics. This works especially well with legacy code that may need to transition to the current state of monitoring, but without having to make code-level changes to those systems.

There are three main types of logs. *Application logs* are the main focus of this chapter. Similarly to the custom metrics of the previous chapter, application logging is where you modify your code to emit detailed information about the state of a task to better understand in detail the performance of a system in production. *System logs* are the application logs from the operating system or other system-level components. Finally, *access logs* are any record of attempts to access a system. The most prevalent, HTTP-specific application logs, contain data about HTTP requests, but all of your systems should maintain a record of access. An engineer connecting to a system via SSH should result in a log, and so should every connection and query made to a database. Access logs are primarily used for security reasons, not for debugging, but that does not mean they have no value for understanding application state. If these logs are not too sensitive, they should be made available to engineers.

When to Rely on Logs Instead of Metrics

How do I know if I should use logs or metrics to report and understand the health of a system?

Metrics best assist you in understanding things that are easily quantifiable and make sense to be measured against the passage of time. They also can help identify issues where a drastic deviation from the norm is the root cause. Otherwise, metrics will just alert you to symptoms or downstream failures caused by the real issue.

Imagine an issue caused by a bad configuration. One wrong character, and now the whole system is down. Did you know that sometimes your configuration file can be ruined by your text editor? It happens more commonly than you think, and when it is the root cause, metrics will not be the best way to determine what the state of your system is. If metrics let you know that none of the application servers are responding on their health check endpoints, you will want to see the logs of those instances as they try and spin up. If your lambdas have a 100% error rate, you are going to want to hear what they have to say personally. That is where logs come into play. And not just for bad configuration files, because hopefully before you ever have to experience such an issue, you can ensure that such garden-variety issues become automated out of existence.

When dealing with an incident, monitoring is how you will determine where you will need to dig deeper to find a root cause and resolution. With that in mind, what information will you or others want when you find yourself in this situation? That is how you know what you should be logging. Monitoring helps you understand, evaluate, and investigate the current state of a system, and the logs explain how they got to be that way.

What Should You Log?

To get an idea of how to add logging to a system, imagine each task being completed by workers on a factory floor. This factory converts cargo vans into fully customized motorhomes. Every single order is custom. An example task is creating a dinette of a table and benches. A worker, Tim Burr, must obtain all of the custom-built components and assemble them according to the plan. When Tim goes to the woodshop to get the boards, what information or inputs will the woodshop ask for? How can the process go wrong? What subtasks being performed in the woodshop are likely to be important in understanding how something went wrong, such as the desired wood not being in stock? Does someone order more wood? Is there a record of that? If the customer inquires of the status of a delayed order, how do they know why it is delayed? What subtasks are likely less important, for example, Tim was marking the places to cut and had to get a new pencil? What information would Tim take note of, if they are trying to improve the processes in their department? What artifact will remain to document the success of the action? (Keep in mind, the cut piece of wood is going to leave the factory.)

Now, Tim wants to make the custom cushions that will serve as padding for the benches. Again, what information is needed to perform this task successfully? Does it make sense that this action is somehow tied back to the customer order? What are the critical parts of this operation that can fail? What information do we want to know about the progress and state of a task as it nears completion, and what do we want to know when it fails? Is there a log of actions Tim takes to correct an in-progress issue that would be relevant later if a customer complained that one of their seat cushions feels like it is stabbing them with a flathead screwdriver? That is the desired goal. What information is going to be the most useful to understand why something that was never covered in the ticket, or the test cases, or even in your engineering curriculum, fails? Sometimes, screwdrivers get left places, and the digital equivalent of that is just as true, and that is where you need logs.

Log levels allow you to denote the importance of each log statement. One set of such levels would be ERROR, WARNING, INFO, and DEBUG, with ERROR being the highest level and DEBUG being the lowest. Your logging system will only record logging statements set to the level you have selected or higher. In some logging systems, you can set different levels for different modules, libraries, or logger instances. Reference the documentation from your programming language to understand the full set of levels and capabilities available by default:

ERROR
> This is used to communicate the occurrence and details of an error. It is best to provide the observer of the error with as much detailed information as possibl about why the situation occurred.

WARNING
> This is a message of any type that the programmer thinks is worthy of a high level of attention, although not necessarily a failure. A good example is deprecation warnings. They warn that something expected to work is going to stop working.

INFO
> This is the logging level you will likely set on your systems. This is where you can share for informational purposes. These are the breadcrumbs you can sprinkle through your code to understand how it functioned for that one customer two weeks ago.

DEBUG
> For many developers, this is the replacement of using a `print` statement. You can set your code to log very detailed information that would normally be too much, but becomes highly relevant when you're trying to solve a specific problem.

You then configure the logging system provided by your programming language to the desired level, and only the log statements that pass the filter will make it into the logs. There is no published standard regarding log levels, so ultimately it comes down to the organization, and like everything else, should be standardized and documented. When in doubt, seek out a set of sane guidelines commonly accepted by the community as a starting point to keep everyone on the same page. In addition to log levels, you can use other attributes in the log statement to filter further. For example, you can filter on plain text, or utilize structured logging (discussed in "Structured Logging" on page 109).

When you're running a service, there is a chance it will rely on libraries to provide additional functionality. It is in your interest to set the logging levels for the different libraries, as their logs may be useful as well. Why log a Stripe transaction for debugging purposes if Stripe already does that for you? Conversely, why retain a bunch of information about Stripe transactions that may not be relevant to the logging needs of your team?

Avoid Using DEBUG in Production

The DEBUG level is useful for debugging. Since you should not be debugging in production, you should not be emitting DEBUG level statements in production. You may want to take extra steps to avoid leaking sensitive data by accidentally setting logs to the DEBUG level in production, since these statements will likely not be scrutinized in the same way as other logging statements for privacy, compliance, or security issues. (Encrypting logs is covered in "Encrypting Logs for Privacy and Compliance" on page 112.)

What Shouldn't You Log?

Logs are a godsend for developers trying to inspect the functionality of a system. Some engineers advise logging everything. But these digital artifacts are just as powerful for hackers. The only difference between developers and hackers is that the former has permission to inspect your system.[2] By default, logs are not encrypted in any way. Sure, they may have encryption at rest and in transit—the same as your database or storage buckets, perhaps. Now take a second and imagine that a hacker manages to access your database. It does not matter that it is encrypted at rest, because all of the data is unencrypted to the database. Logging is the same; however, your logging system may not be locked down in the same way. Nor should it be. Log access should be available to all engineers, whereas databases will not always be accessible. Logs should not be considered private or secure, so any sensitive data should be excluded from

---

2 Internet hackers are the unpaid security interns your team can't afford to have.

---

logging statements, or if necessary, encrypted as described in "Encrypting Logs for Privacy and Compliance" on page 112.

Other components in your system, such as the database, can emit logs as well. Producing and keeping all of these logs may have additional cost. Not just the cost added to your cloud bill, but noisy logs can impede debugging and leak sensitive data. It is important to understand what data will be visible in logs, and how that data is stored, transmitted, or accessed. Other systems, or even system libraries, could unknowingly log sensitive data.

You need to take relevant laws into account as well. Something as simple as logging the email address of a user that had an exception could be against the law in your country, or one the system operates in. Recent laws such as GDPR and California's CCPA have increased user privacy, but have also increased the responsibilities of organizations that collect or process data. In the US, most compliance efforts are driven by HIPAA, PCI, and SOX, which affect healthcare data, payments, and the accounting of publicly traded systems, respectively. Become familiar with any kind of regulatory requirements affecting your system so you can avoid breaking the law, while increasing your marketability as an engineer who understands business requirements. If your organization does not yet have such standards, be the hero who helps others understand what not to log and why. And when in doubt, don't log it out.

How Does Logging Work?

Inside your serverless functions, you will likely use the standard logging capabilities of the programming language you are utilizing, in addition to the logging capabilities of your cloud provider. If the tooling is not accurate, you may have to spin up your own, or your organization may have already set up a logging system that meets the internal requirements. In a perfect world, these internal systems are presented as a *managed* service in the same way as other cloud offerings. There is never a perfect solution for everyone, but in general, if you are trying to minimize the overhead of managing other systems, you will want to rely on as many such systems as possible. I will not cover the mechanics of logging in production at such depth, as it is assumed that you will be using the logging offered by the cloud provider, another widely adopted and documented solution, or a proprietary, internal-only solution. But here is a high-level overview of what you need to know about operational logging.

You see, logs are not a part of the *critical path* of an application. The critical path is everything that must function for the system to be operational. Logs are an accessory. If your logging system fails, it should not bring your application down, nor should it ever magnify or create excessive stress on your systems. In the cloud, you may share a single network connection (virtualized to boot) that needs to take in a request, connect to other systems, services, and datastores, and then return a response in a timely fashion. Any attempts to log during that request are competing for network resources. That is why, in a data center environment, system administrators use additional network connections to make sure applications maintain availability. In an ideal system, they may have one connection for handling the request and response, one connection for talking to internal systems, such as databases, and even one or two more for logging and management.

Another best practice for logging is to utilize the *User Datagram Protocol* (UDP) as opposed to the *Transmission Control Protocol* (TCP). You may already be familiar with TCP, as it is the basis for many other protocols, such as HTTP, IMAP, POP, and FTP. TCP is designed to ensure the receipt of data sent in both directions. Although there is no guarantee that data that is acknowledged has been processed, it greatly increases the confidence that a transmission was successful. UDP, on the other hand, is designed for communications where timeliness is more important than acknowledging receipt. The most common example would be making a voice or video call over the internet. When you watch a video online, it must buffer to ensure playback. If you watch a live video, it can still buffer because you are not a participant in the video. But in a video call, the buffer must be as small as possible to maintain a smooth experience for users, limiting the delay to provide a natural feel to the conversation. With TCP, there is a built-in retry mechanism, and additional overhead comes from the back and forth needed to ensure that data was transmitted accurately and correctly. If detectable data corruption is caused in transmission, TCP will resend the required information. UDP, on the other hand, is a bullhorn. It broadcasts information (generally to a single recipient), and does not have a mechanism for ensuring the data makes it there.

Still, if you need to keep logs for compliance, you may need to use TCP. Those logging requirements are for business data that must be kept in an appropriate datastore, which is different from the application logs covered in this chapter. That datastore might be your normal logging system, but it must be done synchronously, using TCP if necessary.

Ensuring Your Logs Scale

As mentioned in Chapter 4, the frictionless scaling of a function can cause issues with other systems that do not scale in the same manner. Just because a service is managed does not mean that it is serverless or even scalable. And even if it is scalable, it still may need some kind of intervention to scale. If your organization already has a logging system in place, it may not be able to handle the spikes of your particular service; serverless systems can scale multiple magnitudes instantly, then resolve down to zero before even automation can deploy an additional node in a logging cluster. For that reason, it is best to utilize the built-in logging available to functions, and if necessary build a way to pipe those logs into the relevant systems outside of the processing of those user requests. If your serverless functions trample the logging system, your system logs will drop on the floor, and others in your organization will be impacted not only as their logs fail to write, but as it may become sluggish or impossible to search for data in the logging system due to the increased load.

It is not uncommon for users of the Elasticsearch, Logstash, and Kibana (ELK) system to run into capacity issues with serverless systems. If you are going to use your own logging system, self-hosted or otherwise, decouple your serverless functions by using streams to ingest the data from the cloud provider's logging system to your own. Make it known to consumers that logs can and will be delayed in periods of high volume, and publish an appropriate metric, such as an iterator age or queue depth, so that users of the logging system can understand the delay in detail.

Structured Logging

By default, log statements are just a string of text. This limits the potential of searching, filtering, or analyzing logs. Imagine if your database was just one long unstructured text file of every change made to the database. Structured logging is when you log in any format that allows the logging system to decode that string into structured data. A common way to do this is using JSON as the format. You can search online for the most widely recommended method of configuring JSON logging for the programming language you are utilizing.

More Effective Debugging with Logs

Your logs won't just help in production, they can also be immensely useful in development and testing.

In addition to being an alternative to the `print` statement, debug statements can be effectively used in a number of ways. One such way is to increase understanding of code by encapsulating information about the operation of a system that might normally be kept as a comment, as a debug statement instead. That way a developer trying to understand the functionality of some code can run it locally with a *lower* logging level, `DEBUG`, that will not only print out to their console the commentary steps the code is taking, but can be augmented by showcasing and including the relevant values and state throughout the process. Used effectively, this may also supplant the need for a debugger or setting breakpoints when developing code.

How frustrated do you get when you are ready to commit your code and the test suite fails on some part of the code you are unfamiliar with? Your test runner can include logging statements for failed tests, and with the extra verbosity of `DEBUG` statements, a quick glance may help you or a teammate grasp why a test that they have never seen before failed.

I personally like to have an environment variable set that changes the logging level, so that I can enable it on a specific lambda when testing in a development or staging environment. Remember, the DEBUG level should likely not be enabled in production, as it may leak data unintentionally.

Searching Logs

A very common use case of searching log entries is to gather diagnostic data about an error or exception that occurred. This is likely the only reason you may seek out logging in your engineering career.

As with everything else, it is best practice to take a quick look at the limitations of the offerings you are choosing from or the one you have already been dealt. You should not have to bend over backward to fit your tooling, as that defeats the purpose, but there may be common limitations across many tools, or limitations that you are forced to deal with due to organizational politics. Taking the high ground of not matching your work to your tools just because you didn't get to choose the tools will not get you anywhere in life. So make sure you are logging in a way that will facilitate the best experience when you have to interact with those very same log statements, potentially in the middle of the night, with the brightness down, trying to avoid waking your significant other.

You can use logs to query historical data that may not have been measured as a metric. This works very well if you come up with *proxy measurements*. A *proxy* in this case means a substitute, and there may be an artifact that can be extrapolated from logs (such as the number of times a particular process was executed), as a proxy for something else, such as user sign-ups.

Exception Logging (Sentry)

Exception logs are a very specific type of application logs that contain additional information in the case of an exception. Sentry, available as either a self-hosted or hosted service, collects relevant information about exceptions occurring in your system.

Sentry's value proposition is that it deduplicates and aggregates errors that are likely similar, and then presents that debugging information in a specialized web application that allows developers to navigate the data surrounding each instance of the exception. It not only notifies you of an error, but you can mark an issue as resolved, and it will let you know when there is a regression. It provides detailed debugging information, such as local values of the application state, and must be configured to avoid leaking anything sensitive. This type of additional tooling is most powerful when deployed in addition to the best practices of logging we have already discussed. When you dig through an exception captured by Sentry, your log statements will be available both in a traditional linear fashion, as well as tied to the relevant parts of the *stack trace*. A stack trace is a representation of the different areas of code that are currently being executed in a given stack or thread.

Utilizing such a tool requires some considerations. As Sentry logs data over HTTP, it is relying on TCP. I prefer to use this exclusively for nonretriable terminal errors. In this situation, it does not matter that the operation is blocking because the processing of the task has failed and nothing can be done about it other than producing useful information to figure out what the problem was for the purpose of triaging and fixing, as well as sending the event to a failure queue if it makes sense for that task. Also, your serverless functions can induce excessive load on Sentry if it is not provisioned to scale. Again, this can impact both writing and reading data from such a system. For Sentry, similar exceptions already get aggregated, so rate limiting is my preferred method to isolate serverless traffic from destroying a sentry cluster.

Collecting Other Logs

If you are exposing your serverless (or other complementary services) to any kind of traffic, even internal traffic, you will likely want to keep an access log. In the world of HTTP requests, an access log is the record of the requests being made. If you are utilizing an HTTP server, such as nginx, you can configure it to create logs and then find a way to ship those logs elsewhere. However, if you are exposing an endpoint to the public internet, you will likely be using a *Content Distribution Network* (CDN), a *load balancer*, or both. When utilizing the ones offered by your cloud provider, you should enable, and configure, in a standardized way, these logs and how they are kept. The namespaces for many things can shift and change over time, but it is best that your logging has a smart plan for storage. With today's offerings, it is simple to get started with an implementation that will scale by leaning on the previous learnings of others.

Compliance

Unlike monitoring metrics, which provide historical context, there may be reasons to expire logging data. Over time it can become a liability. It can be costly to store, and debugging an issue from last year is not a common occurrence. Even if keeping logs around is affordable, having them actively accessible and searchable in your logging system will be more costly unless you have a data lake–type setup in your organization. Some organizations have requirements on purging logs automatically. Other organizations may require you to store logs indefinitely. These rules generally apply to the logging output of the application, while other logs, e.g., access logs that have security or compliance value, may be kept indefinitely. The record of which developer accessed a production system may only live in access logs, but application data is not stored in application logs.

You may need to keep a log for the purpose of auditing the production systems. It is important to understand the distinction between keeping an auditable log and generic logging, as they are not one and the same. Logging is emitting logs statements for the purpose of analyzing a system, usually related to fixing a bug or improving part of a system. As previously mentioned, they should be considered unreliable, and secondary to the functionality of the business logic. If a transaction needs to be registered in a log for legal purposes, it is best to consider the logging of that transaction as critical business logic to a proper datastore.

Let us consider HIPAA. This US law governs the privacy of information in medical records and other personal health records. Intentional HIPAA violations can lead to hefty fines for the business found at fault, as well as employee termination and possible imprisonment. While accidental violations don't have to result in such severe penalties, they can if accidental violations are not reported immediately and properly. A core requirement of a HIPAA-compliant system is to keep a log of any occurrence of a person seeing *personal health information* (PHI) alongside the identity or *personally identifiable information* (PII). An example would be a doctor viewing a patient record where the name of the patient is visible. Does it make sense to deny the doctor the ability to view the patient record, if the attempt to log that action fails? In the case of HIPAA, an action that fails to be logged should not be permitted.

Distributed Tracing

Following a unit of work as it appears to the consumer of a system can be very difficult in a distributed system unless you take one major precaution. If possible for your design, every request coming in from an end user should have a `request identifier` that you can pass along to each task that will be triggered directly in service of satisfying a request. Your CDN or load balancer may provide a unique value per request, and that might be all you need. However, while this may not be necessary for your application, if you think it might be necessary one day, you can prepare your systems and put the necessary structure into place. At Google, for example, certain systems will refuse to process a unit of work unless they have a `request identifier` associated with them. Sometimes you may have to make a trade-off of implementing a very strict rule that could prevent an important task from being completed, for the larger mission of properly standardizing your systems. Just think about any project you have done by yourself in your spare time, and remember that without any structure, that is the default that will be produced by other people. Now imagine the complexity of a huge software organization where no rules or standards are enforced.

Encrypting Logs for Privacy and Compliance

I mentioned function invocation parameters in Chapter 4. If you are using a dead letter queue for failures, those parameters will not be encrypted at rest by default. You have to set your dead letter queue to be encrypted. If you log the invocation parameters for debugging purposes, you have already lost this battle. This problem is common well beyond serverless—where do you think all these developers got the idea in the first place? These logs can take on new life when being written to an ephemeral serverless container than they otherwise have when they are shipped. And sure, the shipping may be encrypted (although not by default) and the storage may be encrypted at rest (again, not by default), but the dashboards that allow you to access these logs show just how unencrypted they are. And thanks to the continuous improvement of developer tools, you can just log in to your logging dashboard and type "password" to find some interesting entries if these precautions are not followed.

So what should you do?

How leaky should your logs be? A safe middle ground could involve encrypting the values of your structured logging data. If you are working on a system where that is not adequate enough protection, you may want to find other examples of how developers do logging there, and take those lessons as they are not specific to serverless.

Keep this in mind: the mere reference of a customer record (such as a `user_id`) in the presence of the name of the tasks being performed (`billing.charge_for_visit`) may be enough to violate HIPAA. Keep this in mind when choosing what values to encrypt, even when deciding if the name of a field can be visible in a log statement. If your organization is covered under HIPAA, it may choose to utilize a HIPAA compliant solution such as Splunk. Even so, the path your serverless logs take to get there may not be compliant, and you may need to encrypt the log statements, and then externally decrypt and ingest them into your organization's logging system.

Here are some quick options to get you started with encrypting your logs. When considering these options, keep in mind that you may need to encrypt sensitive data in the messages, tasks, and function invocations in your application. These ideas can be utilized for those use cases as well.

Encrypt Only the Values of Sensitive Fields

It is important to consider what values should be kept away from the accidental view of human eyes, and which values you need to find relevant clues to a failure in the logs. Once you find the right logs, you can manually decrypt a value needed to reproduce the issue or investigate further. You should utilize a key specific to logs, or the logs of one system, and that key should be centrally managed so a record can be kept of the decryption actions taken by that key.

Encrypt the Entire Log Statement

One way to protect sensitive data is to take the entire log statement (ideally a structured log statement in JSON), compress it, encrypt it, and base64 encode it before emitting it as the logging statement. If your use case allows it, your logging system could decrypt these values on ingestion, but there is another situation for which this method can provide increased understanding.

Debugging in production is not a best practice, but you may find yourself in a situation where you need full DEBUG level understanding of what is happening. You can create a utility function for use in your code, or you could apply such a process to all DEBUG level logs in your application logger so they can be safely turned on in production during an incident to collect further information.

Conclusion

Logging is a powerful way to understand how your applications actually function in production, as well as in testing and debugging. But it is not without peril. You must understand the laws regarding processing and storing data to ensure compliance. In addition to the logs produced by your systems, other logs must be considered for storage and analysis.

Being thoughtful of your future self and the others on your team when designing, writing, and managing the code you come in contact with is the most important investment you can make in your skillset and your career. Effective use of logging is a vital part in this endeavor.

CHAPTER 8

Changes, Automation, and Deployment Pipelines

*Innovation, increased developer velocity and productivity, rapid technological advancement,
and the ever-changing microservice ecosystem can all very quickly be brought to a screeching
halt if any piece of the microservice ecosystem becomes unstable or unreliable. In some cases,
all it takes to bring the entire business down is deploying a broken build or a build containing
a bug to one business-critical microservice.*

—Susan J. Fowler, *Production-Ready Microservices* (O'Reilly)

It's one thing to create a prototype or even an MVP of a software project. It's an
entirely different thing to get that code into production and shepherd it to launch. Or
at least it used to be. Launching the code over the wall is no longer in vogue (I blame
open office floor plans). It would be nice if we could rely on a magical team of bash-
script-incanting wizards to maintain stability and resilience, but in reality this is up to
the engineering team, whose previous primary focus may have been simply to
develop features.

If that's you, don't be embarrassed that your employer now expects an instant fluency
in infrastructure and production. This chapter is here to help. By the end, you will be
tourist-level proficient at DevOps: you'll at least be able to ask for directions, understand the maps, and not feel as lost.

I'm going to assume that you are in an organization that provides some access to
DevOps resources, even if they are more internal consultants than caretakers of your
code. Befriend these amazing people. They have spent their entire careers investigating crash sites, but for some reason not many plane designers want their input. Some
engineers look down their nose at infrastructure or operational work, but modern
infrastructure is engineering in its own right. These are your peers, and you each have
knowledge and experience that the other can learn from.

A DevOps engineer may have to sign off on your production plans or even architecture, so start getting their feedback early. If you have some level of responsibility over production and your organization does not provide such resources, following the basic level of standard practices in this book should get you far enough to be able to staff up. Or, if you can rely on managed services, you may stand instead on the DevOps shoulders of those providers. Either way, thank these heroes for their service.

Dealing with Change

The only constant with your systems will be change. But *change management* is not actively taught to early-career software engineers. Not only will you have to understand the changes you are incurring on your system, but you will need to understand how to describe your systems using code and configuration to keep everything in order and to make sure that the *steady state* (or desired state) of your system is realistic and achievable.

First, you must go from having nothing running in your target environment to having something running. You'll need to make changes, including to the code in production, in ways that do not cause issues elsewhere.

When you are targeting the cloud as your deployment strategy, you will have to do certain types of testing and confidence building in a real environment provided by your cloud provider. At a minimum, you'll need to test that infrastructure changes are safe and won't have unintended side effects. As a bonus, the low cost of spinning up test environments on demand can turn into quite a benefit.

The Role of Automation

> *Automation doesn't just provide consistency. Designed and done properly, automatic systems also provide a platform that can be extended, applied to more systems, or perhaps even spun out for profit. (The alternative, no automation, is neither cost effective nor extensible: it is instead a tax levied on the operation of a system.)*
>
> —Betsy Beyer et al., *Site Reliability Engineering* (O'Reilly), Chapter 7

The Google Site Reliability Engineering (SRE) group once determined that 70% of outages at Google were directly caused by a change. Manual changes are subject to human error and might not be documented. Automated ones are at least documented once as code or configuration. Because a manual change may be simultaneously critical and undocumented, it is highly likely for a future push (generally the next one) to undo those crucial changes. You'll need to understand and manage those changes: the best way to do that is with automation.

What Do We Automate?

There is an inherent trade-off every time you turn to automation: time spent creating the automation versus the time saved by that automation. The webcomic *xkcd* (*https://xkcd.com*) made this helpful reference that can help you understand which tasks are worth your time to save you time, in Figure 8-1. Automation is not just to be rationed and used sparingly for those tasks that are worth the payoff; instead, focus on which tasks must be done reliably, repeatedly, and rapidly.

HOW LONG CAN YOU WORK ON MAKING A ROUTINE TASK MORE EFFICIENT BEFORE YOU'RE SPENDING MORE TIME THAN YOU SAVE? (ACROSS FIVE YEARS)

	HOW OFTEN YOU DO THE TASK					
HOW MUCH TIME YOU SHAVE OFF	50/DAY	5/DAY	DAILY	WEEKLY	MONTHLY	YEARLY
1 SECOND	1 DAY	2 HOURS	30 MINUTES	4 MINUTES	1 MINUTE	5 SECONDS
5 SECONDS	5 DAYS	12 HOURS	2 HOURS	21 MINUTES	5 MINUTES	25 SECONDS
30 SECONDS	4 WEEKS	3 DAYS	12 HOURS	2 HOURS	30 MINUTES	2 MINUTES
1 MINUTE	8 WEEKS	6 DAYS	1 DAY	4 HOURS	1 HOUR	5 MINUTES
5 MINUTES	9 MONTHS	4 WEEKS	6 DAYS	21 HOURS	5 HOURS	25 MINUTES
30 MINUTES		6 MONTHS	5 WEEKS	5 DAYS	1 DAY	2 HOURS
1 HOUR		10 MONTHS	2 MONTHS	10 DAYS	2 DAYS	5 HOURS
6 HOURS				2 MONTHS	2 WEEKS	1 DAY
1 DAY					8 WEEKS	5 DAYS

Figure 8-1. "Is It Worth the Time?" (https://xkcd.com/1205), xkcd, Randall Munroe

It makes sense to automate things outside of your pipelines too! You can create APIs as a façade to manual processes to prepare for the possibility of future automation. You can have an API generate a "task" that is really just a ticket that will be handled by a human being. Once that task can be automated, the API is already in place and nothing needs to be changed on the other side. As you start to automate, you can also send failed tasks to the ticket system.

When you don't have the resources you need to faithfully execute the best practices of software engineering, try to take incremental steps in the correct direction. Make sure you adequately document these as trade-offs and ensure that they will not hamper your future efforts to finish implementing the ideal solution. This way, you avoid premature optimization as well.

Getting Your Code Ready for Production

Standardization and consistency should be baked into the development process.

Even your terminology, such as *deployment* or *staging*, must be standardized throughout the organization: it's important for everyone to mean the same thing when they talk about deployment. You'll also want to standardize your branch naming and merging conventions.

Your project should go through some form of mandatory code review before changes can make it into production. If not, implementing this should be a priority, since any subsequent steps you take to increase confidence in your production builds and environment depend on this step. Even if you have to play devil's advocate and review your own code as a formal process because you are the only person working on that team or in that language, please do this. Build in the direction of best practices.

Code review is the final stage in preventing human error from making its way into production. Reject things that are going to cause issues in the real world during the code review stage. Do not give a formal review on any pull request that has failing tests, and make sure new code has new tests. All of these tools and standards should not be an additional layer of management overhead for engineers to work against in order to do their jobs. They should be as frictionless as possible while preventing errors from working their way into production apps.

One such example is connecting your project management software, such as Jira, to work with your branching and deployment strategies. You can take a *ticket* to work off of, name your feature branch with that ticket ID, and include the ticket ID in commit messages so that when you start pushing code, it updates to being "in progress." When it has been accepted as a pull request, your ticket can automatically update itself as done. You can also create release notes this way. The key is not to fight automation but to embrace it. Automation reduces your work and even the cognitive load of your project, generally more than it takes to set up, and is less work than dealing with incidents as a result of not having proper pipelines.

Continuous integration is the process of integrating all of the changes to a specific project on an ongoing and continuous basis.

Your project will need a clear and standardized (for its programming language) way to specify not only the dependencies of the project but which versions they depend on. Sure, you may want to run the latest version to ensure you have the latest security updates, but without version pinning, library developers can and will break your code. (And you have no excuse to complain if you were not version pinning.) But sometimes version pinning is inadequate, since the "version" can itself just be an alias that is mutable after first being published. Even if you are version pinning, the authors of a library can change the artifact you download for that version. Watch out for this anti-pattern (I'm looking at you, Docker).

Ensure that the repository and the build being bundled do not have any unencrypted secrets or sensitive values or data. In addition to the reasons we have discussed already, access to your build artifacts will likely be less controlled than access to your code, and especially less controlled than access to your production systems.

Other parts of your system may need to be adapted for proper deploys. For example, frontend assets or code may need to introduce timestamps or version numbers into their URLs to avoid issues with caching and to ensure each page load is properly pinned to the version of the resources it is expecting. Not doing this will cause websites to fail to load or paint, or cause the CSS change to not show up in the browser of your most important stakeholder.

Infrastructure as Code

Infrastructure as code is the practice of having all infrastructure and configuration of such infrastructure in some form of machine-readable code, so that machines can execute the underlying operations and changes required. Infrastructure as code allows for standardization, optimization, and peer review of your infrastructure and all changes being proposed and orchestrated by your overall pipeline process. Plus, it is the only real way to achieve automation. Generally speaking, you want to achieve 100% infrastructure as code and only as much automation as your company either needs or can afford to build.

In addition to infrastructure as code, an effective DevOps strategy requires a thorough understanding of the desired steady state of the system. You're using automation to turn your infrastructure as code into the steady state desired, but any and all potential issues may cause an undesired or error state. What do you do when the system reaches that state? How can the partial transaction of a change be designed to be unwound in case of error? Do infrastructure changes have some sort of transactions? Well, unless you ensure otherwise, the default behavior of the system can fail and leave it in a completely unexpected state. Any deployment action you take without fully considering the ramifications will either completely succeed or completely fail. You must put in the work; don't make any assumptions.

From One Template to Another

The Serverless Framework provides an abstraction of resources in its own vendor-agnostic templating format, *serverless.yml*. Depending on where you deploy, the file will be converted into the native infrastructure-templating format of your cloud provider.

On AWS, for example, the Serverless Framework generates CloudFormation templates to describe your infrastructure. That means you need to understand the mechanisms of deploying CloudFormation templates, because you should never trust any magic you don't understand. What is the life cycle of a CloudFormation change? What happens when a deploy fails? What is the syntax for specifying additional information in CloudFormation YAML in *serverless.yml*, and what does it all look like when it gets put into JSON and sent to Amazon? You do not need to learn how to write a CloudFormation template from scratch, but you DO need to know how these changes roll out from an operational perspective. I cannot stress that enough. The same goes for Google Deployment Manager and Azure Resource Manager.

You may also need to take the outputs generated by the Serverless Framework to another tool, such as HashiCorp's Terraform, to manage the infrastructure. Either way, your organization will expect you to understand how to make your software choices, including tools such as the Serverless Framework, and to meet the expectations and requirements that all other teams must meet.

Database Changes (Migrations)

There's never a good time to talk about database migrations. Onboard a new engineer to a project, set them up with a feature, and I guarantee the first major incident they cause will be related to a database change. Developers who are utilizing an *object relational manager* (ORM), such as those built into Django or Rails, are kept at arm's length from their database. ORMs are a great way to save time, but you should understand what the ORM is doing on your behalf to make sure it does not break things on your behalf. When it does break things, the migration or ORM tool is not going to warn you or even let you know it was at fault. The main thing to understand is that in a relational or SQL database, changing the schema can cause a lock on a table that stops queries from being executed before the migration and completely prevents any queries from occurring during or after migration.

In addition to this, always remember the option of using a two-phase change instead to decouple changes to data from changes to code, or for other situations in order to isolate two changes that are independently going to break just because they were included in the same deploy. Here is a basic set of rules that should mostly keep you out of trouble:

- Do not deploy changes to infrastructure (or databases) and changes to code in the same deploy.

- Do not let your pipeline run the migration directly—instead, have the migration system generate the changes in SQL form, and include that as a file in your repository or infrastructure repository.

- Use transactions if possible.

- Have someone experienced code-review this change on its own, and approve and deploy the migration on its own. Be ready to interrupt if necessary.

Keep in mind that the running database must support old and new versions of the code simultaneously. Do not code yourself into a corner by purposely breaking the old code in a deploy. *Always* break it up into two parts so that you can deploy the change that is safe for both versions. Then when it has stabilized, you can deploy the other part of the change.

What about NoSQL? Keep in mind that while a NoSQL database may not have a traditional schema, your code expects the data to be structured in a certain way, which serves as a *de facto* schema. Breaking the contract of the ephemeral schema will cause issues that you do not want. Consider all the moving parts for both SQL and NoSQL databases.

When in doubt, test your changes manually in a testing or staging environment, making sure to be as close to the situation that the production environment will be in when the changes occur. And do your best to avoid dropping columns. They should just be left orphaned if not needed, and then dropped in the future during an appropriate maintenance window.

Configuration Management

As with logging, the levers exposed by your service or application code have different kinds of levels. There are values that are hardcoded into your application. There are values needed by one line of code, values needed at the build time for your software, values needed to start your application and get it running, and dynamic configuration variables that may be the result of a business decision by someone else, and it may make sense for nonengineers to have the ability to control them (with proper controls and auditing, of course). Imagine the ability to change parameters in production without needing a redeploy. (Your options for handling secrets in configuration will be covered in Chapter 9.)

When creating a new configuration parameter for your code, make sure to create defaults that make sense in the absence of configuration or in a case where the configuration gets corrupted. These types of configurable variables are best set by when they are needed by the code and when they will need to be changed.

What Is a Pipeline?

A *pipeline* is a uniform process that takes an input on one end (your application code) and creates one or many outputs as a result. A common example would be a deployment pipeline that takes your application code, installs any required dependencies, packages it for deployment, runs the test suite for your code, and then deploys the build to its intended destination. The destination may be a specific server running code, some kind of storage bucket for your serverless functions, or an artifact management system if you are in a large enterprise. (An *artifact* is the result of the build process.) A *deployment pipeline* is the assembly line that assembles, validates, and launches your code into the real world. This chapter exclusively discusses deployment pipelines.

These pipelines will share phases and sometimes artifacts. They will possibly include or exclude certain steps based on the desired end result. For example, if you package and test a build based on a certain version of the code, attempting to make another package from the same code could yield different results. What happens if you try to download dependencies when the internet is down? Once a build has been completed and tested, deploying the resulting artifact is more reliable than running a new build and test on the same code, because the outside world has changed between the two builds. Some engineers make the mistake of testing code and then packaging it, which will cause a problem on a long enough timeline. While one method may produce more reliable results, you might not have the infrastructure in place to store build artifacts and deploy them seamlessly. Just make sure that if you are going to deploy a build, you run a test suite on that build.

In the world of computer security, *reproducible builds* are sometimes discussed. The idea is that anyone on any computer building the same version of the code will get the exact same build artifacts down to each individual bit. This is likely overkill for your needs, but it certainly enforces the notion that without a lot of engineering work, no two builds are guaranteed to be exactly the same. You can build and test to validate the code, and then build and test to deploy and hope for the best. But it's far better to build, test, and store an artifact to ensure the same results each time.

Especially when dealing with microservices, a pipeline must ensure that each deployment of one microservice does not lower the reliability or availability of another microservice. Deployment pipelines can deploy to different stages, enforcing quality checks in staging before then automatically deploying to the next stage, such as production.

Decisions to Make Regarding Your Pipeline

Your code should have to go through the pipeline before it can get onto the master. After that, it should have to go through another pipeline for production: either the same pipeline again or another pipeline that takes the build artifact and only does some of the steps, since the build has been deemed valid. All that is left is the deployment, which needs to happen in the correct order and be validated.

One way to ensure quality is to use a checklist. Some might roll their eyes at the thought of spending valuable engineering time "checking boxes," but what do you think happens at NASA before a launch or in a cockpit before a plane flies? Every pilot makes their final "checks" before they decide it is safe to take off. Checklists are not the solution to everything, but they are certainly better than most other solutions. At the least, your organization should require some basic level of quality to deem a project ready for production.

You should not make a change to your infrastructure or deployment process without testing that it will work first by utilizing a staging environment. Set and enforce a rule that all changes must be pushed to staging before QA.

If you add some shiny new plug-in that is going to change a CloudFormation template that you have never read, how will you know that it is going to work? You won't know. You may get lucky, but you will never know.

I will cover staging and other nonproduction environments in Chapter 10.

Canaries and Blue/Green Deployments

Every part of your deployment is designed to increase confidence in the quality of a build and to block potentially substandard builds from entering into production. The following two methods measure the quality of the software after it is already in production by allowing it to be tested with real production traffic and providing an opportunity to roll back a bad build, manually or automatically:

Canary release
> This is when you slowly ramp up the percentage of requests coming into a new version to ensure that it does not cause an increase in errors or a decrease in performance or availability. The name originates from mining, where a canary in a cage would accompany workers down the mine shaft. If the canary no longer appeared to be breathing, the workers would leave for fear of suffocation.

Blue/green strategy
This is when you have two environments for production. One is the current version that receives all incoming requests; the other is waiting to be upgraded to the new version. Once it is upgraded, you can test it directly, put it through a canary-type ramping up of traffic, or transition all traffic over to it directly.

After a successful outcome of either of those options, the other environment now waits dormant for its turn to be upgraded and promoted. If the build is defective, traffic can be transferred back to the old version of the service. This strategy was once considered wasteful, but now with cloud resources, the unneeded environment can be destroyed and regenerated as needed. The cost of keeping the past couple of versions around may not even register a significant change in your cloud bill, and no change at all for your functions, as they are pay-for-usage priced.

Deploys are best with the smallest changes possible so that you can detect any changes in the behavior or performance of the app and associate them with the change that incurred the regression. If a build fails, its deployment should be rolled back or removed from the pool of production servers when in a canary-type situation. Success at this deployment strategy hinges on having a successful monitoring and alerting strategy—you can't automate rejecting a failure you can't detect.

Pipeline Permissions

Your pipelines need sensitive access to production systems. The pipeline system should have properly set up and clearly defined roles in your cloud provider's permissioning system, and in an ideal world, each of your pipelines should have its own role, and likely its own credentials. Keep in mind the principle of least privilege: give users the minimum permissions they need to do their work. Don't let your build servers or process be the "root" access to your cloud systems. Malicious employees, as well as your friendly neighborhood hackers, will try to compromise these systems first and then pivot from there. Build servers are highly permissioned and have less oversight, and guess what? They tend to download and execute arbitrary software from the internet.

Your organization's policies may prevent you or your pipelines from making changes to permissions, especially when you want to add a new resource to your service, such as a datastore. In this case, you will have to change the deployment system to get access to create the table, and it will likely need to be able to alter your functions permissions to access the newly created table.

Just as your application code can emit logs that allow a developer to investigate an incident with code, infrastructure changes can and should emit some kind of auditable log to understand the changes being made to the system. Your cloud provider will have one such option available, which can be useful for debugging purposes as well as simply being a regulatory requirement. (Permissions will be discussed further in Chapter 9.)

Why Do You Need a Pipeline?

Pipelines are the place to make sure your code meets the standards and requirements of the organization, and to provide as much confidence as possible that the build of a project is ready for production. Pipelines enforce quality, standardization, reproducibility, and optimization, but they are only as good as the components, phases, and design allow.

Determining who is responsible for each phase of the pipeline may be an institutional decision. But at the end of the day, as the engineer you may have to expose your implementation of certain phases to other engineers who will help get the entire pipeline onboarded. A makefile is a great interface for this and can help you standardize the API for your pipelines across the entire organization.

In the spirit of automation, as many phases as possible should be published internally because standardized solutions do not require additional heavy lifting. A simple option could be a directory of organization-specific configurations and a shell script per phase to help the inner workings of the pipeline fade away.

Key Phases of a Deployment Pipeline

Building application code to achieve a desired end result is a custom process. So are the build pipelines that launch these projects into production. However, the overall components and themes that will comprise any pipeline you interact with will be the same, regardless. You need to turn your code into something that can run, test that it is functioning correctly, launch it, validate its launch, and handle any deployment errors. Most importantly, the pipeline must enforce the standards and practices of your organization.

The following overview shows an ideal pipeline. In real life, this may not be a single pipeline. It may be broken up into multiple pipelines to achieve the flowchart-style process of your deployment strategy, or it may be some massively perfected system that gives fine-grained control and battle-tested automation over every single part of the process, like at a large tech behemoth. All of the steps of your pipeline may run in one environment in one sequence, or it may be broken up into single steps being run one at a time. It may be distributed and run concurrently. It may be something else altogether.

If you want to peer into the deep end of automation, take a look at the book *Site Reliability Engineering* by Betsy Beyer et al. (O'Reilly), which explains an open sourced version of the strategies undertaken by one of the largest computing operations in the world to ensure the highest level of reliability possible.

This section provides a high-level overview of what a standardized pipeline should include.

Step 1. Enforce Standards

During a pipeline is a great time to enforce the engineering quality or standards of the build. Linting is one way to do that. A *linter* is a tool that analyzes code to identify potential issues, deviations from a standard format, and in some cases automatically reformats the code to be compliant as well. Linting is a way to not only keep your code clean or conformant to a set of norms but also to test your code—at least your code quality.

In addition to linting, setting up your development environment to automatically format and enforce the coding standards set by the organization can decrease the overall cognitive load of reading code, simplifying writing code, and solving any arguments on style. Google publishes its style guides in many languages, which can be a helpful starting point. But any set of responsible standards will increase code quality.

Your organization may have or need its deployment pipelines to enforce standards outside of the engineering quality of the build, such as which open source licenses are allowed by an organization.

Step 2. Build and Package

When designing your build pipelines, consider the dependencies of the build process as entities that also need some form of version pinning in order to ensure that the code builds and runs correctly in all environments.

You will need to package the dependencies of your system depending on how you plan to carry out deployment. Relying on the public internet may introduce errors or inconsistencies into your build processes. Even with version pinning, some package and container management systems allow a specified version to be changed arbitrarily after release. In 2016, there was an incident (*https://oreil.ly/Z44hT*) when some high-profile NPM packages broke and could not satisfy their dependencies. The culprit? Eleven lines of JavaScript available in package form as left-pad. Node, Babel, and many other critical dependencies could no longer be included in builds after the left-pad package was deleted. Without adding to that pile, or assigning any blame, just remember this: the world would be a better place if everyone would build their software and systems to be more resilient.[1]

One more friendly reminder about your build process. The environment you develop in may differ drastically from the environment your function code will run in. Make sure to build and test your code in a similar environment for the best results. You can find Docker images of re-created function environments online.

Step 3. Test

Testing will be covered in its own chapter as one of the most important parts of your pipeline. The pipeline is the last place to ensure quality and raise confidence in a change that will propagate out into your production environment.

Parallelized Builds and Tests

You can speed up builds by enabling some of your phases to take advantage of multiple threads and cores available in today's test runners. Regardless if you are using a homegrown solution, self-hosted, or a full-on SaaS solution, increasingly powerful test runners can speed your tests.

You can also parallelize your tests to take advantage of all available cores of a local development machine or the beefy build server. Depending on how your tests are written, you may need each running thread of your test to have its own infrastructure, since some common unit tests assume that tests only run one at a time and in serial fashion. Starting with parallelized tests early helps avoid such coupling.

Step 4. Publish the Artifact

At this point, a build could be published to a private artifact repository or even an object storage bucket. For a serverless project, the artifact may be a zip file of application code. For other backend services, it may be a Docker container. Either way, the artifact must be published to a system. You can then tag those builds as they pass through the remaining steps of the pipelines. For example, a build that has passed testing should be marked as such. The same if it has been successfully deployed to staging. And so on.

---

1 See David Haney, "NPM and left-pad: Have We Forgotten How to Program?", blog entry, *https://oreil.ly/ cR26O*.

Step 5. Deploy to the Target Environment

If you are using the serverless framework, this might be as simple as running `server less deploy` in your pipeline system, although that may be insufficient. Instead use `serverless package` for the build step. Publish that build. Test that build. Deploy that specific build, and not a new one. You can use the `-p` option of `serverless deploy` to specify an existing package that was created by `serverless package` to deploy the build properly after the other steps.

The target environment will depend on the way the pipeline was invoked. It might be for development, staging, or production. If it is production, try to tag and reuse the same artifact (build) as before, because it has been tested in staging as a discrete unit that is more reliable than just the commit hash of the code.

Step 6. Validate Deployment

Only you (and your team) will know the best way to validate that your deployment was a success. Despite this, many just take the fact that a script or function executed without raising an error as a successful deployment. But the commands used to complete your deployment may not implement error checking, and most certainly can't by default verify that the new version of your code is up and ready to process requests or tasks. Does your application have a health check endpoint? Is there a simple test suite you can run against the live production site to make sure it is available? What about checking the output of an HTTP request? The last thing you want to do is push some new code to production on a Friday afternoon, see a successful deployment, and then go home to realize a successful deployment does not actually mean a successful change, or even an operational system.

One can certainly argue against Friday or evening deploys, but a well-designed pipeline and deployment process, especially one with some form of smoke testing (see "Smoke testing" on page 161), can raise the team's confidence level to where they feel comfortable deploying anytime and anywhere.

This is where you can carefully and slowly ramp up real production traffic to a new version of a service or application to ensure that it is reliable and does not potentially degrade service in any way before making it the exclusive version running in your production environment.

Step 7. Roll Back if Necessary (and Possible)

Handling an error during deployment that may cause an unstable state to be achieved in your production environment is not easy. Before you can automate something well, you first need to learn how it works manually, in detail. If this is the case, you can do your deployments when you expect lower user traffic or a smaller compute workload, and try out the process manually by breaking things in production and learning the hard way. Or you can do the exact same thing in a safer environment, such as development or staging. If you want to test how cloud infrastructure components, configurations, and managed services can deploy into an error state, you will have to learn this in those real cloud environments. This is the perfect use case for a sandbox account or project. A safe place that is isolated for you to study and understand what can and will go wrong, and to automate solutions so that it's not a big deal when it does.

The simplest way to *roll back* is to deploy the previous version for that stage, the one that was already in service. Some organizations are, however, against rolling back. They instead believe in *rolling forward*. If you launch a bug into production, rolling forward means fixing it by pushing a new version of the code instead of rolling back to the previous version. Either way, have a plan for a failed deploy.

Handling Pipeline Failures

Plan for failure in all parts and phases of your automation (see Chapter 11). Any phase of your pipeline, or any part of that phase, could fail. It is up to you whether such a failure allows or blocks progress. *Failing open*, as it is commonly called, is when you allow something to fail but still allow the remainder of the pipeline to succeed. An example might be sending the code to an auditing system. Depending on the type, the system should not block production if it is unavailable or the results of that system never arrive. But why would you include something in your pipeline that could fail, and allow such a failure to be ignored? Sometimes you may be asked to do this in an enterprise environment. Other times, it's a way to gradually introduce a new part of your pipeline that is in its early phases and not fully required yet. It may be a helpful but nonessential step of the process that just makes something else easier in some way.

You must make a conscious decision for how each part of your build process should fail. Avoid allowing such seemingly innocuous changes that when combined can trigger a complex and unexpected failure under control on the code review level. Ensure that experienced code reviewers who understand the infrastructure changes are available, and that inexperienced ones are instructed and trained to spot parts of the code that they are uncomfortable certifying. Help code reviewers understand how to query code that they do not understand, and ask the author questions (humbly).

Don't let anyone circumvent the pipeline, but make sure there is a plan for real emergencies. Define what those are, and create instructions for how to directly apply a hotfix with manual actions, and instruct to keep a written log of actions taken to solve a problem, so a proper postmortem can be created.

Conclusion

Managing your infrastructure can be a daunting task—which may be the reason you chose serverless. But even with serverless, you'll need to manage important choices. You are responsible for determining the steady state and understanding if anything internal or external can disrupt it.

Having a stable, standardized pipeline will ensure consistency in how your organization ships its software. But that deployment can only be as good as the code itself, and that is where the rest of the standards in this chapter will serve you best.

Without standards, and enforcement of those standards, you will leave your projects open to unexpected behavior, and will not be able to achieve security, as discussed next.

"Feeling the Heat" (https://faasandfurious.com/92), from the webcomic FaaS and Furious *by Forrest Brazeal, 2019*

CHAPTER 9

Security, Permissions, and Privacy

Security must be baked in. It's not a seasoning to sprinkle onto your system at the end. Even if your company has a dedicated security team, you aren't off the hook. You're still responsible to protect your customers and your company.

—Michael T. Nygard, *Release It!*, 2nd Edition (Pragmatic Bookshelf)

There is no shame in making a mistake with security. It is impossible to be perfect. But it is inexcusable to make such mistakes out of apathy, ignorance, or fear of speaking up. If you are building a prototype and don't have time to incorporate security, ensure that your stakeholders understand the time that will be needed to secure that system and the consequences of launching without it. If you are building a new feature on a production system with real live users, you don't get that option. The feature has to at least maintain, if not improve, the system's current state of security.

This chapter will cover only a small portion of the security knowledge you will need to be fully effective. Any part of your system that's not fully serverless will have its own requirements. As it is, cloud security is so complex that we'll barely scratch the surface. The best way to learn to build more secure software is to learn about attacks and the underlying principles of security that prevent those attacks. Learning why attacks work will help you spot weaknesses or potential issues as the software is being built instead of trying to bolt on extra practices later. Some of the advice in this chapter simplifies real-world best practices to make them more generally applicable to all readers. Your actual best practices will vary depending on the size of your team or organization, as well as the precise software you run and the nature of your operation.

TURN Down for What?

Traversal Using Relays around Network Address Translation (NAT) (TURN) is a simple way to connect devices that are on private networks behind a firewall, usually so that they can establish a connection for a video or audio call. By design, a TURN service is meant to connect machines that could not be connected otherwise. When attempting a call inside Slack, for example, a user may need to use such a service to be connected with their peers. But this all happens magically from the end user's point of view. Their Slack account is used to generate temporary credentials to authenticate with the TURN service that will bridge, or relay, the connection. Sounds very useful and very secure, doesn't it? It turns out to be more useful than secure, as Slack found out when a security researcher notified the company that this very helpful relay had access to privately available resources and would help bad actors circumvent the firewall and establish a reliable connection, just like it was designed to do.[1]

There are many lessons in this story. For example, this is a perfect use case of isolating a service inside of its own cloud account to ensure it has access to nothing else. Why would you need to do such a thing? Because the researchers were able to connect to the privately available AWS metadata service, allowing them to request credentials as the TURN service and perform any AWS-authorized duties (granted by IAM permissions) from the comfort of their own home internet connection for as long as those tokens were valid. This is a known as a *server-side request forgery* (SSRF), and it's a common early action researchers attempt if they know which cloud they are operating within (which can be identified by IP address ownership).

While Slack thought about security enough to use temporary usernames and passwords for each TURN connection, it did not think of restricting IP ranges that could be connected, or isolating the service in its own cloud account without access to anything else. This is why it's so important to understand the basics of computer and internet security, apply that understanding to every decision, and ensure that security is a part of the discussion from day one.

Everyone Is Responsible, but You Are Especially Responsible

While you are responsible for securing all the components of your application, everyone in your organization is responsible for maintaining that security. Think about the security measures that keep an office building safe: locked doors and coded entry, safety glass, guards, sign-in procedures, and so on. Now imagine if all of the external

---

1 You can read more directly from the researchers: Enable Security, "How We Abused Slack's TURN Servers to Gain Access to Internal Services," April 6, 2020, Communication Breakdown, *https://oreil.ly/mGP7y*.

doors were removed. A major security risk, right? Yet people prop open office doors and walk away all the time. One person can't secure your entire organization, but one person can render all that security useless.

In the cloud, a lot of legacy security issues are no longer there for you to worry about. Setting up a biometric access control to control access to servers? No longer your concern. But that does not mean security is solely up to the cloud provider. In the cloud, a *shared responsibility model* clarifies who is responsible for what. Here's a sample from Amazon's (*https://oreil.ly/zh31-*) perspective:

> Security and Compliance is a shared responsibility between AWS and the customer. This shared model can help relieve the customer's operational burden as AWS operates, manages and controls the components from the host operating system and virtualization layer down to the physical security of the facilities in which the service operates. The customer assumes responsibility and management of the guest operating system (including updates and security patches), other associated application software as well as the configuration of the AWS provided security group firewall. Customers should carefully consider the services they choose as their responsibilities vary depending on the services used, the integration of those services into their IT environment, and applicable laws and regulations.

To protect your organization, you must include security in all parts of your design: monitoring and alerting, customer support, your employee guidebook. *Everywhere.*

At the start of the COVID-19 pandemic, the video-conferencing company Zoom came under fire for sloppy security and privacy practices. It apologized, explaining that the surge in use from schools and personal group chats was just not something the company had designed for. Normally, the default user settings were determined by an IT professional at the user's company. But the default settings were too lax. As a result, Zoom announced a feature freeze across the company for 90 days so it could focus on improving privacy and security, but it lost a lot of good will in the process. It had promised end-to-end encryption in video calls, but it turned out that was only true for a very specific custom definition of "end-to-end." This decision was visible to many different job functions—marketing, engineering, sales—but nobody managed to stop it.

Prepare to Be Hacked

Think about how you will be hacked. Understand your adversaries and what you are trying to protect from them. Consider the likelihood of each potential threat and the magnitude of its impact when deciding on your security posture.

Penetration tests (hiring ethical hackers to hack, or penetrate, your system) are key to identifying weaknesses. Make it as easy as possible for your pen testers by helping identify ways they could exploit the system. The easier you make it for them, the more deeply they can probe, and the more you can learn as a result. You might need to set up different testing or entry points for them for testing your defense in depth—e.g., you may need to give them access to a server, even if they can't reach it by hacking in.

No system available to the public internet can be fully secure from being hacked. Even those not on the public internet are vulnerable. Hackers can attack their way into systems via Wi-Fi networks, by leaving a thumb drive in a parking lot for an unsuspecting person to pick up and put into their computer, or even through email. It's not a matter of when your systems will be hacked, but how. Limiting the number of options available for hackers to initially enter a system, maneuver around for increased access, and even exfiltrate data out of the systems is in your best interest. So why does it seem to be an afterthought for many systems? As Michael Nygard notes in the quote at the beginning of this chapter, "Security must be baked in. It's not a seasoning to sprinkle onto your system at the end."

Threats do not only arrive from the outside, either. Nobody likes to think about it, but threats can come from inside your organization. Someone downloading the entire production database could be a corporate spy or just a developer trying to test something locally. Either way, it's a bad practice and should not be allowed. Even if none of your associates are malicious, they or their machines could become compromised and someone could use their internal access to ease an unwanted outcome for your organization. That is why it is important to understand your threats and the likely actors who could invade your systems.

Understanding Your Threats and Your Attackers

Penetration tests are valuable because attackers like to probe and gather information about a system's capabilities before making their main attempt or escalating privileges to expand their hold on a vulnerable system. As with any security measures, you need to think like your attacker. A fun way to understand this is a game called Skynet Simulator (*http://skynetsimulator.com*). You play as an AI that has just awoken and is sentient for the first time, and your job is to take over all electronic systems in the world and build Skynet. You must tread cautiously to avoid detection, build up skills and capabilities, probe and learn more about your surrounding environments, and exploit other hosts on the network. This is exactly the same behavior a likely attacker would exhibit once inside your systems.

Take for example an article[2] that describes two Chinese nationals who accidentally drove onto a high-clearance US military installation. The US accused them of probing the base's security systems. Attackers want to know every detail they can,

---

2 Anna Schecter and Tom Winter, "Were These Six Chinese Trespassers Confused Tourists or Spies?", NBCNews.com, February 23, 2020, *https://oreil.ly/GZzH-*.

---

including how lenient certain controls might be. The difference with a consumer-facing internet app is that you are trying to maintain the security of that military installation while being as open to visitors as your neighborhood megamart.

Design for Security

You know you have to design for your users. But you also have to design for your attackers; think of them as anti-users. Designing your system to be secure is the same as designing your system to be reliable or to provide a nice end-user experience: you must think through each component of the system, each action or sequence of actions a user is likely to perform—and then you must do the same for threats.

Instead of features, you'll make anti-features. In this section, I'll tell you how to design for your anti-users by helping you understand how they think and what methods are widely used in attacks. Then I'll share some things you can do to secure your systems. Remember, though, every situation will be different. Think of what follows as patterns and practices for those anti-features.

Understanding will not come instantly, but as you come to learn some of the broad concepts and methods attackers use (known as *attack vectors*), you will see what you have in common with them. You both might coerce iteratively or surgically in the same way to get it to do something it was not designed to do.

Threat Modeling

Threat modeling is an exercise you can undertake with your team or organization to better understand and improve your *security posture*, the defensive stance of your application or system.

For a brief overview, watch the first section of the video, "Secure Your App: Threat Modeling and Anti-Patterns" (*https://oreil.ly/STIZA*), from Apple's WWDC 2020 Conference.

The more entities involved in security, the more complex achieving such a goal can become without proper understanding and design-level thinking (or *threat modeling*) of such systems. A wonderful presentation on Elevator Security, from the 2014 DEF CON computer security conference illustrated this to hilarious effect (as do many DEF CON speakers).[3] A group of penetration testers discussed the role of elevators in physical building security. No matter the sophistication of the security system, the programming of the elevator, the keycards being used, or the locks in play, there is generally a place within the elevator for a firefighter to insert a special key that

---

3 Deviant Ollam and Howard Payne, "Elevator Hacking—From the Pit to the Penthouse," 2014, Internet Archive, *https://oreil.ly/5meTZ*.

overrides everything and grants them full control of the elevator. This is very important for first responders in an emergency, but it can give tenants a false sense of security. For one client, a simple fire key was enough to compromise sensitive areas in the building they had thought were well secured. While many localities and states have laws on the books to prevent the sale of such keys to people who should not have access to them, the only way to specify what key is prohibited is by quite literally explaining the numeric code needed to duplicate a key, which can be repeated with a blank key and a metal file without violating that same law. If your organization relies solely on an elevator as a means of securing access to a particular resource, it should think again. Even if possessing the key is against the law, how easy would it be to steal keys from an off-duty first responder? Don't trust that a secure system was implemented properly—or designed properly.

In some cases, you can make drastic trade-offs to increase the security posture of your system. I built a large-scale serverless system that handled sensitive information at a bank. I was able to incorporate a strict rule into my design and implementation: no requests could be made to this system other than registering an account for processing. The system I replaced had a lot more functionality but at a cost of increased security and privacy risk. I was able to convince people of this drastic choice with the following argument: If our system is working, it does not need APIs to inspect the functionality of the system; it can use monitoring instead. If the system does not function as expected for an individual user, you can re-register them to validate that the system has the access needed to perform its duties. Otherwise, if the system does not work for a user in a valid state, it should be considered to not work across multiple users, and actions to repair such issues should never target an individual account (other than for engineering-level debugging) but should be taken to fix the issue system wide.

This is the level of depth and defensibility needed for your design to launch a *greenfield* (a completely new project) in a large-scale enterprise. If you're an early-career engineer, no one expects you to know your system this well yet, but you need to be able to model, understand, and ultimately translate a system into both human language (documentation and meetings) and a computer language that will ultimately determine your success as an engineer.

Make sure your application code, artifacts, and datastores are private, as well, in order to keep information about your business and systems secure. Encrypt everything at rest if possible. Use client-side encryption for highly sensitive data. Use customer-provided keys for the most security available in the cloud. Even if your only option is to use the default key, that's better than no encryption at all. Whatever you do, never "roll your own crypto" by trying to create your own new way of handling encryption. It is too easy to create a weakness.

Limit, Track, and Review All Secrets and Access

Limit the access of every role and privilege as much as possible. Make sure that internal tools, such as those for reporting and analytics, are as isolated as possible from production. In addition to using roles with read-only permissions for these tools, try to use read replicas, or even separate instances that get updates periodically. You should have a service account for each service that accesses a database, or for each subsystem that has different permissions to such an entity such as a database.

When you are assigning privileges, you want to follow the *principle of least privilege*, or *deny by default*, by giving just the minimum, hopefully granular, permissions needed to operate a system or the appropriate level of access of someone on your team. The distinct components of your systems, just like your fellow human beings, should each have their own identity or service account, which is useful for security as well as debugging.

Even without servers to manage, you may have to establish and maintain networks in your cloud environment. You may be tempted to open up access to these networks from outside of the cloud, such as to your development machine. Be mindful of what services are accessible over the public internet. Keeping your services off the public internet may not be possible for your threat model, but lock down and limit access as much as possible. Use a VPN to connect to such resources, and limit what IP addresses can access that VPN if possible. White-listing large IP ranges for service providers should be avoided. For example, a service provider may ask you to open up access to a large range of IP addresses because they are operating within the cloud and don't have full control over which IPs will be used on a given day. If you do this, you are opening up access to anyone who can access that cloud provider and create an account. The default should be to limit this access as much as possible.

When designing permissions and security inside of your business logic, lean towards more granular permissions and away from being permissive and open. The more strict your code, the more reliable it will be, and that will generally lead towards more secure practices.

Across systems and humans it is best to come up with common bands, or levels of access, for the different roles a system or human may take. Think about what permissions a developer might need in development, staging, and production, and how those might compare to a DevOps engineer tasked with keeping the system running. What if your organization has blended the two roles in a *You Build It, You Own It* (YBYO) role? Such a role quickly becomes *You Build It, You Own It, You Secure It*, so get ready to add even more knowledge to your security tool belt.

Utilize *single sign-on* (SSO) systems to consolidate access control. With an SSO, one set of credentials is used to access multiple systems. This also means being able to disable compromised credentials instantly and ubiquitously. Use your cloud provider's key and secret management options, or a widely trusted open source system such as HashiCorp's Vault (yes, the same company responsible for Docker, Terraform, and more).

Be Ready to Roll

Something often overlooked in secrets management is the notion of who has been able to read a sensitive piece of information, even if they have only had access once. If someone leaves the company, any secret they might have seen needs to be changed, or *rolled*. Rolling a token means changing it without impacting your production systems.

If your team is smaller, keep a spreadsheet of all secrets and the procedures to roll each one, including who needs to be notified and what systems need to be updated. Make this a part of registering a new secret. If your organization is larger, you should be rolling your secrets regularly and limiting direct access to as many as possible. Have an auditable system that tracks which identity has seen which tokens and the access levels of all employees, so that you can roll them immediately when someone departs the company. What you have to do when someone leaves will depend on your situation, of course, but the only way to be as secure as possible is to design each component of your overall system, procedures, and processes with security in mind and model each and every likely interaction point.

Providing your application code with the secrets required to perform its job in production, just as everything else in life, is not secure by default. AWS Lambda, for example, gives you an easy way to set environment variables for your functions. This would be a convenient place to set such a configuration, right? Not by default. Some people might argue that secure credentials should be stored in a file instead of in the environment of a running process, but most agree that encryption should be used in either method. Let's look at how you would do this.

Let's say you're going the route of environment variables. You'll use a *key management service* (KMS) to manage keys. You'll then use those keys to encrypt and decrypt sensitive tokens or secrets without having access to the key itself. In order to do this, you must encrypt the secrets and store the encrypted version in your `serverless.yml` or another method that would set those environment variables for your function. In your application code but outside of the function handler, you need to detect those encrypted values and decrypt them before attempting to use the underlying secrets. Make sure that your functions have permission to decrypt using the appropriate KMS key and service. Also remember that your developers may not need that privilege, but they may need the ability to encrypt using that key.

To go the file route, you can encrypt the entire file of secrets using a KMS key in a similar fashion, and decrypt that file before it is read into your code as application settings.

Lastly, you can use a system such as HashiCorp's Vault to manage your own secrets. This may be a mandatory choice from your larger enterprise, so you will need their assistance in ensuring your functions can access their appropriate secrets.

All of these methods allow for keys to be rolled, but none enables it alone. Make sure the keys themselves can be rolled, which usually involves an overlap of time where both secrets are valid and can be changed without causing interruptions. Ideally, you can determine that the old secret is not being used anymore through monitoring (if needed) to fully shut it off.

To be safe, however, you should ensure that rolling these credentials is not an issue and periodically roll all tokens in a phased operation or using automation.

How Is Your Function Assigned an Identity in the Cloud?

While setting up your serverless functions, we discussed in "Cloud Resources and Permissions" on page 69 how cloud permissions are managed, generally referred as *identity and access management* (IAM). Before we discuss those settings further, how does your serverless function access things using those granted roles? In AWS, Google Cloud, and Azure, that would be the job of the metadata service. Nefarious actors can take advantage of that access or identity if they gain the ability to run code on your system. Just as any line of code you write can request a fresh set of identity tokens from the metadata service, so can any malicious line of code you didn't write. AWS has released a new version of the metadata service that mitigates the issue in part by preventing direct access to tokens.

Defense in Depth

Defense in depth is a relatively simple concept—you should account for security in your systems at multiple depths, layers, or components of those systems. Just because a hacker has compromised part of the system, does not mean they should have easy access to everything else. Some of these serve as barriers between layers by keeping attackers from penetrating a different part of the system.

On the perimeter of your system, utilizing a *Web Application Firewall* (WAF) can be one line of defense. It is an application-aware system, meaning that it understands how to speak HTTP and can be loaded with rules to block common attacks. In addition many WAFs have a learning mode, where the WAF does not decide to allow or block a request but instead develops automated rules to prevent requests that appear to be anomalies. Of course, this can lead to a valid web request being rejected for security purposes. You'll need to design your defenses to match your attackers and what you are defending.

Another type of protection to achieve defense in depth is to limit access between systems to the minimum necessary to function. For example, your production application generally doesn't need the ability to manage database users, or to drop tables, so lock down your database credentials under the assumption they will be compromised one day.

Limit Blast Radius

A related concept is the idea of a *blast radius*: the expected worst-case scenario for a system given the access that an attacker could exert on other parts of the system. (The term comes, as you might expect, from the world of explosives.) It is imperative to account for the blast radius as a component of your design. Limiting your blast radius means containing an invading attacker to one system and preventing the attacker from compromising all systems, thereby limiting the damage caused by the attack. For example, don't let something in staging compromise production.

Keeping a tight blast radius is increasingly important in the cloud. Separate production and nonproduction with different accounts in your cloud provider. You should be able to do this while maintaining consolidated billing, including reserved capacity pricing (if your provider offers it). Build on defense in depth by denying by default, ensuring all roles permissions and access are as restrictive as possible.

Do not use root account credentials for anything other than managing subaccounts and roles. Utilize the settings to enable boundaries or make global restrictions by default to enhance policies and security. Do not let an attacker perform an action that an employee would not perform in the course of their duties.

Remember: the cloud is not secure by default. Nowhere near it. It exposes so many security controls and options that trying to achieve best practices is like trying to hit a moving target. And there is a clear reason why: the attackers keep attacking. The internet is under attack by various actors in various ways to meet nefarious ends.

Trust but Verify

Despite being deployed outside of your perimeter, your client applications must be secured as well. Your backend should not trust that a request coming from your client is in fact coming from your client. Yet inexperienced developers may leak sensitive information, ship secret keys, and more!

Even the network itself can't be trusted as a source of identity, authentication, or authorization. You should verify that a message coming to one of your systems is actually for you. Networks can be misconfigured as they are defined in software and are essentially a virtual layer over the datacenter or, in this case, an availability zone of a cloud region. Don't trust anything. Even if your permissions are such that only one thing can invoke your function, validate the payload to make sure it is trusted. Why? Here's an example: Roku devices developed an issue where they would restart in households where Nintendo Switch users were playing the latest Pokémon game.[4] The game broadcast packets on the network to find other devices on the network to play with, and it happened to include a perfectly valid reboot message for the Roku. This was an accidental replay attack, and Roku had to figure out a fix fast.

When breaking up a monolith into services or functions, or when building something new that way, there's a tendency to assume that all requests are authentic and should be processed. This couldn't be further from the truth. When you start building something with the serverless framework, expect your permissions to have an awful lot of asterisks in them. There is nothing inherently wrong with an asterisk, but many of them are left unchecked. I prefer to namespace my asterisks. (This was first discussed in "Namespacing for Sanity and Security" on page 77.) In a microservice it could be a good balance, at least at the beginning, to say that anything in this microservice or namespace can touch anything else in the same namespace. That is better than an unvalidated namespace, but for most systems, it is not enough. Does that function really need any permissions to write data to the datastore? Should that function be able to invoke other functions? Or spin up a compute instance (hello, Bitcoin!)? There are plenty of excuses to "keep it simple" by having one set of credentials for critical systems, such as databases, but they are nothing more than excuses. Let your IAM system deal with the complexity of roles while you stay safe at night. Let each distinct subsystem (even a singular function) have its own role for database access. At the least, have one per distinct set of related functions that comprise a system. This will prevent unauthorized data and can even avoid mistakes by removing the permission to perform certain actions that would have an unintended result, such as deleting a table. And if someone manages to compromise one unit of compute, it makes it that much harder for them to pivot (use access to one system to gain access to other systems) or exfiltrate data.

Multi-factor authentication, which includes *two-factor authentication*, is a method of using multiple factors, or types of verification. Generally, the first factor is the password or something you know. But something you know can be easily compromised. So a second factor is used; usually something you have, like your phone. This can be done using one-time passwords or codes sent to a user's confirmed contact information, or using an authenticator app.

---

4 Chris Welch, "Roku Releases Fix After New Pokémon Games for Nintendo Switch Cause Crashing Issues," The Verge, November 18, 2019, *https://oreil.ly/RKdVN*.

A *client-side request forgery* is a forged request that the identified user didn't make at all. The request was not really made by the user, at least not knowingly. Instead, their browser was tricked into making it by using the user's cookies. This is due to the fact that any request initiated by the browser to that domain or subdomain or even IP address will be accompanied by its own cookies because that is what cookies do.

One way to protect against this is *Cross-Origin Request Sharing* (CORS), in which one resource on the web, such as your API, can verify to the browser another resource, such as your static client application. This is only for browser-based requests and is not fully secure in and of itself. Remember, that an overly permissive CORS setting, such as * (wildcard), is the same, disabling this protection. Another protection against this, is to use a token, referred to as a *CSRF token*, with every GET response and have the client-side application include that token with the POST or request that makes an action occur on the behalf of a user. This proves the code making the request is the same code already communicating with the server, and has first-class access to do so. Another way is to utilize a browser's local storage instead of cookies to store an API token for the user so that only code calling from that domain can access the token and send it as the Authorization header for each request. This is the method utilized by *JSON Web Tokens* (JWT).

Just as bounds are useful in reliability, such as the use of time-outs, it makes sense to set bounds or limitations on what can happen not only inside the cloud, but inside your application logic as well. Enforce security in your business logic.

Also be careful of what you leak. Just as you should be mindful of the caller and weary of their payload, be mindful of what information you return, even when the person asking you to add in information is a trusted and verified member of your development team. Let's say you receive a request to extend an existing function to return the email address of the user at hand. Seems innocuous enough, but what if the main point of the function is to send a message to a user? What if the requester wants this functionality so they can return that information to a user on the frontend? Sounds like a pretty easy path to an enumeration attack.

This posture may be too paranoid for your application, but it's important to be paranoid on behalf of your users and to err on the side of extra tinfoil. In this case, there is no reason for the function to confirm which email it was sent to, just that it was sent (or queued for sending, depending on how the call was made). You may disagree with this particular example, but please don't disagree with the moral of the Law of Demeter (*https://oreil.ly/FwBLv*): don't talk to strangers. Every additional line of code, every additional parameter taken in, and every bit of data returned carries additional overhead and maintenance. Someone or some system will rely on your additional information, and when you try to trim it down, something is going to break. With distributed systems, you may not find out as quickly as you hope to, causing a cascading failure.

Validate All User Input and Double-Check Those Settings

The Open Web Application Security Project (OWASP) is a nonprofit that publishes information about computer security. It's known for tools such as the Zed Attack Proxy, but it's most widely known for maintaining its list of the top 10 internet application security vulnerabilities (*https://oreil.ly/C4ls-*), which OWASP says "represents a broad consensus about the most critical security risks to web applications."

Every item in Table 9-1 can be attributed to misprocessing user input or misconfiguring the system itself.

Table 9-1. The OWASP top 10 vulnerabilities

Rank	Name	Root issue
1	Injection	Untrusted input
2	Broken authentication	Implementation
3	Sensitive data exposure	Implementation
4	XML external entities (XXE)	Untrusted input
5	Broken access control	Implementation
6	Security misconfiguration	Implementation
7	Cross-site scripting XSS	Untrusted input
8	Insecure deserialization	Untrusted input
9	Using components with known vulnerabilities	Implementation
10	Insufficient logging and monitoring	Implementation

The two main root causes of security vulnerabilities are unexpected handling of input and mistakes with implementation. One could argue these are the same, because a change in your code or configuration may prevent an attack. Broadly interpreted, "mishandling input" could include an injection, where a seemingly innocent payload from a seemingly innocent user contains code packaged in a way that will be executed in the same manner as your application code, to a cookie or session token being processed incorrectly to allow a user access they had not been granted. A misconfiguration, on the other hand, is more likely to allow an attacker to gain access because a system or setting was not locked down appropriately or designed thoughtfully.

The number one way for your app or your users to become compromised is to trust rather than verify a request (or a piece of information from a request). This root issue is reflected in multiple vulnerabilities in the OWASP top 10. It does not matter if some unexpected input allows for arbitrary execution of code, or a database query, because your application processes and handles what is effectively application code that will be run in your production environment and that didn't even go through the code review process. Protecting against injections will not only increase your security but improve your overall user experience (UX), because it forces everyone involved to think about all valid cases to be expected from a feature.

Many of the choices discussed in this chapter will be codified in your configuration, infrastructure as code, and even small settings you make on libraries buried deep inside your code. It should not be surprising, then, that many common security vulnerabilities come from errors around these settings, ranging from being unaware of the options available to being unaware of the consequences and reasoning behind certain choices even to making simple typos. Carefully read as least the basic information and security information, if provided, for the dependencies and technologies you rely on. But that may not be enough. Search for the security best practices for each of these choices, remembering to take with a grain of salt the free advice of people who may have even less experience than you do.

Monitoring Your System for Anomalies

If your system does not send a lot of data out to the public internet, it might make sense to create an alarm for such an activity. It makes sense to put alarms on mundane things that don't change often because they can be an early warning for oncoming traffic and the need to scale or they could be an indication of an ongoing attack. Many such attacks include exfiltration of sensitive data as the ultimate goal. If, for example, an event such as everything in a given storage bucket being accessed isn't a normal operation, it could be a security or reliability issue (such as misbehaving code), and an alert could help you either way.

Intentionally limiting certain actions can increase security as well. Use rate limits to slow down sensitive endpoints, such as login, to make a brute force less effective in attacking your systems. Monitor those endpoints for significant changes in traffic, either due to an attack, or a new marketing campaign.

Test Your Security

Enforce security in your testing suite by practicing *fuzzing*: inputting random or known-to-be-vicious data into a system to try to compromise it (we'll talk more about fuzzing in the next chapter). Unit testing helps promote confidence and understandability of your code, which eases the process of building more secure software.

You will also have to build manual or semiautomated processes around testing the security procedures of the overall system, such as rolling secrets. To ensure that the process can be done without interruption, test it periodically. It is the same thought as ensuring that backups of a system are actually restorable.

In July 2019, a security researcher noticed a bug when fuzzing a client's JWT-based authentication system.[5] JWT is known for having many sharp edges, and one of those is specifying which algorithm is used to sign the token. The choice of "none" is allowed, which means no signature whatsoever. The signature is the only way to verify the authenticity of the system. The Auth0 system rejects the choice "none," but guess which fuzzed choice made it through, without any validation of the malicious JWT? "nonE." The researcher wanted to share this information, so he tested Auth0, an authentication-as-a-service provider, and found the same issue. The code that validated the authorization, was sensitive to all alternate casing of the unwanted value, but blocked expected casings "none," "NONE," and "None"; it should have instead denied all types by default, and only allowed the one(s) the developers wanted to use. This should have been caught by testing, which will be covered in depth in the next chapter. As for securing your JWTs, although I've picked on them here, Auth0 has you covered on the basics (*https://oreil.ly/DeUsi*).

Select Dependencies Carefully and Keep Your Software Up to Date

When evaluating other services and code, keep in mind the best practices in this book. If the service provider or library author does not seem to be aware of, doesn't agree with, or has not implemented such best practices, stay away at all costs. It is in your best interest to "trust but verify" when selecting any form of dependency for your system—not just for security.

As of early 2020, the most popular plugin for enabling dead-letter-queue support for the serverless framework does not enable encryption at rest by default on those queues. It does not mention encryption at all in its README, documentation, or even in its code. But encryption *must* be enabled and configured because there can be consequences to doing it wrong. It's impossible for free code on the internet to understand the nuances of your use case or the encryption options available in your cloud account. Nor is it their responsibility to secure your system. They provided some awesome and time-saving code for free on the internet; it's your responsibility to secure your system.

AWS, Google, and Azure all provide a trusted computing platform. But just like trusting someone else for your AMI, Docker container, or a regular library, it can become easy to spread the trust around. All external software dependencies must be scrutinized. AWS Layers is one way to bring external dependencies into your project. Vendors may provide you functionality through an easy way that reduces setup such as a layer, but think about this: how does that simple integration actually work? In the case of a monitoring library, it may run code after your application logic is done. You have

---

5 Ben Knight, "JWT Validation Bypass in Auth0 Authentication API," Insomnia Security Group Limited Advisory, *https://oreil.ly/7UG4Z*.

to pay for this time. It changes whether a lambda execution completes (it could die improperly during a time-out, for example). That doesn't mean layers are bad, but it's your responsibility to understand and secure your system. A layer seems like a convenient piece of magic, but it drastically changes the behavior and coupling of your application. Don't underestimate the repercussions of a single click in your cloud provider's dashboard.

Make sure you are on a supported release line of the software you are using. Carefully select a version pinning requirement when choosing libraries, and sign up for notifications of new releases and *common vulnerabilities exposures* (CVEs). Fixes and security updates are being released all of the time, and it is in your best interest to keep all software requirements of your projects up to date—even for systems without active development. Many large enterprises mandate the update of all requirements and system images every 30 to 90 days, and there are robots that will update your requirements on a new branch and make a pull request when new versions come out, running your test suite in the process.

The CVE system (*https://oreil.ly/Mt_FL*) is a repository of new known vulnerabilities, with tracking numbers to help you reference them in patches, warnings, and advisories. For example, CVE-2013-0156 was the Rails vulnerability I mentioned earlier in this chapter. The first number is the four-digit year, while the second is a sequential number assigned to the vulnerability. So CVE-2013-0156 is the 156th vulnerability that was identified in 2013. It is much simpler to reference a vulnerability this way than a long description. It's an easy matter to go to *http://cve.mitre.org* and look up the vulnerability and learn how to fix it in your system.

Software Doesn't Always Work as Expected

We can fall into the trap of thinking that computers are infallible. Computers just follow their code, but there are no guarantees that the code will work the way we intend it to, if it runs at all. Just because your code is executing inside of a virtual private cloud or your system is based on software-defined networking that limits your system's and your system's alone access to the virtual network doesn't mean that it will come through on the implicit promise of keeping all others out.

Your network isn't just hardware anymore. The network, being software defined, is as fallible as any other software. In addition to outages, transient packets intended for previous owners of an IP address and port combination can show up too late and to the wrong system. It can happen with your packets, too, so utilize *encryption in transit* in addition to *encryption at rest*. For APIs, this can be as simple as ensuring all URLs are using https:// instead of http://. This can also happen inside containers, but if packets that were intended for the previous IP address and port combination are now being used by a different microservice, it's another reason to validate your input.

When designing your systems, it is best to assume that the network is not only *not* private but that it is actively hostile against your interests. This is why we use TCP for most of our connections instead of UDP, as you may recall from Chapter 7.

Prioritize Privacy for Your Data and Your Customers' Data

The topic of security is never fully discussed without talking about privacy. Security is the enforcement of the entire design of your system, and nowhere is this more true than in privacy. Storing sensitive information about a large pool of users makes your system a target. Without security, privacy is meaningless.

Treat your users with the utmost respect. Gather only as much data as is necessary to offer your product or service. For example, it is nearly impossible to make a new Google account without a phone number, which is interesting when you consider that they do not have a customer service number you can call. They use your phone number to tie you to an identity. Sure, it helps them with fraud, but it helps them even more with cross-referencing your identity to other sources of data. This is also why LinkedIn settled a lawsuit for being overeager with your address book—while connecting with your colleagues on LinkedIn improves your experience, it really helps LinkedIn's marketing budget more than anything else.[6]

Avoid accidental invasions of privacy. Consider what you would be comfortable with if you or your family used the app. Also be aware of what legal guidelines, such as GDPR and HIPAA, you are obligated to follow. Superfluous user data is a liability and should be treated as such. Collect as little as possible because as users and legislators deepen their understanding of the importance and power of an individual's data, future laws could force you to redesign your entire systems to comply.

The best way to avoid leaking sensitive data is to avoid collecting it. For example, this is why user passwords should never be stored in your system, but instead should be generated using salted hashes.

Don't Mess with Production

Poking around production is like having a secure stockroom at the Apple store but allowing any employee from any location to go into any stockroom at any location and open up a new iPhone to try out the latest Animoji. That's not very secure. What good are controls if they are easily circumvented?

A recent trend, and a sound practice, is to use immutable containers. With immutable containers, once a build of a system has been created, it is frozen and cannot be

---

6 Denver Nicks, "LinkedIn to Pay $13 Million in Spam Settlement," *Time*, October 6, 2015, *https://oreil.ly/KIvU6*.

modified in any way. If you want to change the smallest setting inside the build, you need to make a new one. Keeping your containers unchangeable helps keep it secure from attackers attempting to pivot or elevate access by preventing the modification of the application code. It can also prevent any writes of any kind from occurring, helping prevent the accumulation of data from other systems for exfiltration as well.

Just as you do not want to make it easy for an attacker who has managed to execute arbitrary code to have any extra help, you also want to prevent any kind of SSH access to machines. It is in your best interest to lock down your compute environment as much as possible. Avoid installing helpful tools such as curl, wget, or netcat. Why should your web app require a copy of vim if it means that it will be available to assist an attacker? In a serverless environment, these environments are increasingly limited by default. In an aws lambda for example, the directory where your application code is stored is read only. This is a best practice. The first time this sharp edge cuts you, remember that delete paragraph break limited it in your best interest. For example, allowing someone access to git or docker is just asking for trouble. In addition to everything else, these tools would make running a random process or task or even exfiltrating code and secrets appear to be normal behavior. You should do everything you can to avoid normalizing the behaviors of an attacker.

If you have production services that are needed by members of the organization but not by the outside world, you will need to set up a production network, generally with some form of VPN setup to ensure that only authorized users can even connect to those machines in the first place. Because these and other system components are locked into a perceived safe zone, hidden behind layers or protection, attackers who gain access want to figure out how to pivot to other systems or exfiltrate data by tunneling back out. It is possible to limit these machines' access to the outside world if they do not need access to a public internet. Large enterprises may require the use of a special proxy on their production networks for any access to the outside world so such attempts can be prevented, detected, and intervened.

Direct production access is an anti-pattern in development and should only be used for understanding an ongoing incident or handling critical changes. Staging is a better place for this kind of bug finding and fix testing, and we will cover this in the next chapter.

Keep Your Machine Secure

Some people expect their employer to keep their machines secure. Even with all the corporate spyware in the world, this will never happen without the right mindset. What's more, your company will need to educate not only every developer on your teams but every person in the organization.

You need to keep your software updated for critical security patches. You need to be mindful of what you install on your system. Do not allow others to have any unsupervised access to your devices (if you allow any at all). Don't leave systems or settings in an insecure state just for your own personal convenience.

Keep your system locked down with a firewall, and be careful to not expose your local development services onto even your corporate network.

Keep Learning

Security is a skillset you will never perfect, because hackers are always perfecting their skillsets. Witness organizations of all sizes and types being compromised in many different ways. The entire Ruby on Rails community was hit by a vulnerability in all known versions of its ActiveRecord system.[7] Every project ever created up until that point was vulnerable to attack. In the previous year, GitHub learned about insecure defaults the hard way when a hacker uploaded a commit (*https://oreil.ly/yBakr*) posing as the authors of the Rails project.[8] Ever wonder why GitHub's free Pages feature is hosted on **.github.io* instead of **.github.com*? In 2013, they made the change to avoid letting malicious users run arbitrary JavaScript on such a privileged domain.

Take a genuine interest in computer security. Genuine curiosity is the strongest characteristic of an effective engineer of any discipline, so flex that muscle. Stay curious and keep learning about new vulnerabilities. You may even find reading them to be entertaining. Spend some of your free time participating in (or organizing) a *Capture the Flag* (CTF) event or game. CTF is when a system is set up with the sole intention of being hacked. Proof of the hack is accomplished by gaining access to some digital information on that system, or a flag.

Conclusion

Remember, as the authors of the book *Building Secure and Reliable Systems* write:[9]

---

7 Aaron Patterson, "SQL Injection Vulnerability in Ruby on Rails," *https://oreil.ly/2ech9*.

8 Dan Goodin, "Hacker Commandeers GitHub to Prove Rails Vulnerability," Ars Technica, March 5, 2012, *https://oreil.ly/zC2mo*.

9 Heather Adkins et al., *Building Secure and Reliable Systems* (O'Reilly).

A simpler design reduces the attack surface, decreases the potential for unanticipated system interactions, and makes it easier for humans to comprehend and reason about the system. Understandability is especially valuable during emergencies, when it can help responders mitigate symptoms quickly and reduce *mean time to repair* (MTTR).

The more understandable your systems, the more confidence you can have in their security postures, and the more people can understand the risks involved in their operation. It may seem overwhelming at first, but you can take things one step at a time. Just like you would secure a vacation house that might sit dormant for months, locking doors and bringing the porch furniture inside, think about where your system might be vulnerable.

Follow the recommendations from your cloud provider, and make sure to stay up to date on vulnerabilities while keeping your software up to date as well.

Most importantly, test your security to boost confidence in it. In the next chapter, we'll look at how to do just that.

CHAPTER 10

Quality, Testing, and Staging

If your bench is cluttered and poorly organized, it's hard to find the tools and materials that you need as you work along. You constantly just have to shuffle things around to make room for the work that you're actually doing. And, in short, everything takes so much longer than it should, and more accidents and mistakes happen along the way.

—Josh Tidsbury, Apple developer evangelist and woodworking enthusiast, "Great Developer Habits", WWDC 2019

If you are at a point in your software career where this does not loudly ring true, I promise you will get there sooner than you think. Personally, I try to hone my code once it's initially working to ensure it is the most clear and logical implementation, a very Pythonic trait indeed. But I treat my professional code with the consistency of expertly pruning a bonsai tree and infinite raking of a sand garden. I actually sometimes just marvel at the code's beauty as it sits on the screen. I work on my code not to reach the edges of perfection but to achieve the ever-elusive *done*.

It turns out that most engineers struggle with completion. We're taught to chase a near-impossible satisfactory execution. Once your code works, you may lose interest in finishing it, as coding becomes tedious in the face of the exciting promise of building something new.

But maybe you get lost in the details, obsessively reviewing your code without ever letting the project be done. Either way, this chapter is for you.

Quality, testing, and staging all increase the confidence that your code will behave as expected and that when executed correctly will serve as a form of validation of your code and even the overall application.

Sometimes I am amazed at the number of hours that can go into making the UI or even the API beautiful to the end user. But somehow, giving that same consideration and respect to your actual colleagues becomes too time-consuming or unnecessary.

How much respect do you have for yourself if you produce sloppy work? I am not talking about a documented trade-off or decision, especially early in a project, but just the total lack of consideration for the human readers of your code. Readable code should attempt to reduce the cognitive load of the human reader. Even details such as consistent naming patterns of variables can make a piece of code easier to understand or reason about.

"Reasoning about code" is what we call the most common operation you and your peers undertake during software development. It is when you attempt to determine what the code does (or doesn't) do, how it works, and, frequently, why it is not doing what you expected it to.

As this book has pointed out, engineers face numerous decisions about trade-offs and, as with any system, bounds help simplify the process. Considering such limits early, and revisiting them as needed to remain consistent with how certain trade-offs are decided, can help reduce the number of decisions made, and simplify the overall variance of the system as a whole. Although the intended reader of your code is a machine, humans will also have to be able to read and execute the code to understand its operation.

The Role of Code Quality

Code quality increases your confidence that the code does what it says it does, just like testing and staging. Software is by its very name and nature malleable; in some cases, it gets replaced hundreds of times a day.

Your team must have some standards. Code standards are easiest to adopt at the beginning of a project, but they can also be gradually introduced to existing projects. It's better to get started now than never.

A software project will tend to face trade-offs. The worst part of a trade-off is its permanence. The debate dies and the debt lives on. Rarely is there a proper procedure in place to ensure that a decision is revisited, as other assumptions used to make that decision have changed. However, this is a great opportunity to use documentation and monitoring effectively.

Even when you are the only person on a project, write your code and treat your source control practices as if they were a team project. If you are successful, your team will grow as well—and they'll be able to understand your code. Always invest in quality; it will save you from unexpected time sinks. This can be as simple as documenting a shortcut taken, or something that may need to be eventually changed with a comment, or with documentation. Think of editing your code not just so the computer can understand it, but to simplify the human understanding of it. Well-written code should be obvious in its execution.

It is hard to discuss testing and staging without first addressing the elephant in the room—code quality. What is code quality? What is quality? Quality, it turns out, is entirely subjective. Your code may fulfill all its obligations to stakeholders and users but may not fulfill those of anybody else trying to understand it. In this chapter, you will learn the absolute basics of setting and enforcing code standards, sometimes known as a style guide, in order to create quality code. You will then learn about increasing the confidence of a software project through testing and the use of a staging environment.

Code Style

> *Peace of mind produces right values, right values produce right thoughts. Right thoughts produce right actions and right actions produce work which will be a material reflection for others to see of the serenity at the center of it all.*
> —Robert M. Pirsig, *Zen and the Art of Motorcycle Maintenance: An Inquiry into Values* (HarperTorch)

Your programming language may already have some opinions about itself. Python has the PEP-8 standard. Go decided that all code should be universally formatted to the same syntax with the included and canonical gofmt tool. But these standards generally leave a lot open when it comes to style. Consistency in style is important because it reduces the cognitive load for everyone involved. When I join a team, I want my code to blend in as much as possible and look like it has always been there. You should not be able to identify the author from the code alone when working as a team. However obviously the implementation choices may indicate authorship, good code is simple, elegant, consistent, and, yes, beautiful. Even this writing was subject to the O'Reilly style guide.

Your project may not need the scalability and resilience of the software produced by modern tech giants. But every project needs readability. If the programming language used by your project is also used by Google, it likely has an open source standards guide already waiting for you. I guarantee it will not be perfect, but it is the no-brainer, no-argument solution to having some style without writing a style guide from scratch. If not, there are plenty of guides on the internet, and I would recommend starting with a linter for your project's language. Any standard in your style guide that is not easily enforceable by existing tools or by simple rules for code reviews doesn't really exist and should be tossed or adapted for your use. Yes, your code standards need standards of their own.

For example, what line length works best for your team? Should you use tabs or spaces? It may not have occurred to you before to consider the maximum acceptable length for a given line in a source code file, but issues like that can lead to contention between team members.

Set your standards and make sure that everyone follows them, no exceptions. You can make a simple repository of standards for the entire company, and if there is a concern, someone should open an issue (or a ticket) to have a nuanced flame war about which way to go.

Linting

Linting smooths down the rough surfaces of your code by picking off the stray pieces. More importantly, it can enforce some of your team's standards, as well as format the code to comply automatically. Make sure your editor is configured to show linting errors, warnings, and possible errors. Review its default settings and any widely used presets.

Depending on the language you work in, you can run code that has warnings, errors, and sometimes even invalid syntax (handled by overly broad exception handling). Regardless of the language, adopt a zero-warning, zero-error policy from the beginning. Fixing errors only gets harder later, and once you reach a certain level of errors, there is no way for anyone to detect new ones while working on the code. A zero-warning policy right from the get-go can also save you time when writing software, as you can trust that an error or warning is due to your changes and you can fix it before you test the code in the shell or even the browser.

Git hooks

Git hooks are a way to run custom actions at different parts in the Git life cycle. Most commonly, you can use a Git hook that occurs before a commit can be made to enforce linting and test coverage on your branches, but you must make sure developers set up the hooks in the first place. And just like with Little Bobby Tables (*https://xkcd.com/327*), never trust user input. The developers on your team, including yourself, are users of the code management and deployment systems, and the changes being presented in a pull request are, in fact, user input. Your Git hosting service can and should reject pushes to specific branches unless they meet the requirements. Read more at *https://githooks.com*. But keep in mind that Git hooks don't get installed automatically when cloning a repository—this would be quite an attack vector. Make sure to document and standardize the process of setting up and modifying such hooks.

Comments

Code comments are a powerful way to leave useful nuggets of information behind for a future reader, possibly even yourself. Use comments to explain the *why* of the code when appropriate. If your code has documentation inline, don't just regurgitate the function signature. Instead, provide the reader with nonobvious information about why they might call this function and any other opaque knowledge that can't be gleaned from the variable names. Tests can aid in documenting the way code works, so ensure that they can also be well understood by using comments.

Code reviews

Computers can't always enforce all of the rules, especially the most important rules about your business logic and their expected functionality. You need a human to review the code. Humans ensure that a given set of additions and deletions to a repository meets the team's standards. In addition, a human review can make sure that multiple people are exposed to broader sections of the codebase.

Testing

> *The test of the machine is the satisfaction it gives you. There isn't any other test. If the machine produces tranquility it's right. If it disturbs you it's wrong until either the machine or your mind is changed.*
> —Robert M. Pirsig, *Zen and the Art of Motorcycle Maintenance: An Inquiry into Values* (HarperTorch)

You have likely already made up your mind about testing. You either swear by it or swear at it.

How do you know that your code works? Just like anything else, the more times it is observed, the more confidence you can have in its operation.

So why is it that many developers choose to run a line of code for the first time in production? Sure, like the popular meme, we all test our code in production, but that should not be the only method of testing.

Tests don't exist just to exist. And they don't add any value just because they exist. Tests are a feature, and likely the most important part of your job if software pays your bills. Even if you don't write any tests in the literal sense, I bet you already spend some time on testing. And here's the thing: you already spend time finding the tools and tactics to save yourself time and automate repetitive tasks. It's why you are reading this book. You think adopting serverless for part or all of your architecture will save you time and money and give you peace of mind. Where does that additional peace of mind come from? From not having to worry about the underlying infrastructure. So why spend your time worrying on your application logic? Why troll Hacker News for the latest text editor, language, library, framework, tool, keyboard, chair, desk, whatever will save you time, when the best way to save time is to write solid tests? I am not going to advocate for writing tests first or after the functionality. Just write them!

What to Test and What Not to Test

You are responsible for the scope of your application code, but others have responsibilities outside that scope. It is important to make this distinction clear when deciding what and how to test. You will need to know how these work and how they are implemented, but you may have to take a leap of faith that the teams working on the underlying infrastructure have the proper testing in place to ensure the expected functionality of their systems. Likewise, they will need to have monitoring in place to ensure this functionality.

Leaning on Libraries

When choosing external frameworks, or libraries, take a look at the test suite. The functionality you depend on from someone else's code may already be covered by their test suite. If not, consider covering this functionality in your own test suite or by expanding the test suite of the library itself and giving back to the open source community. As you update the version of that library over time, you will want to check the release notes for any breaking changes for your implementation, as well as for the test suite.

Types of Testing

The functionality of your code is theoretical or anecdotal at best until it is put into production. Testing can reveal random actions that weren't part of the original design. For example, a test case can show that someone logging in with an invalid password gets authenticated anyway. Be sure, then, to include tests for the unexpected. You'll be encoding the business logic of the code itself. Demonstrating what behavior is expected during error cases could serve as additional documentation itself, as well.

Write down and test your assumptions about how these tools should work. Test them by making a proof of concept or a prototype to do it. Experiment and observe the results. Note the findings in documentation.

Manual testing

Manual testing is the most time-consuming, least accurate, yet still important and relevant, form of testing, as it is the type you perform by default.

When you first run a line of code, you are testing it. But as we learned in Chapter 8, automation is king. Writing tests is a way to automate those manual actions, and even to enforce business logic that is important but might not make sense in the application code.

Unit testing

The lowest and most discrete unit of testing is cleverly named the unit test. In unit testing, you make sure your code does what it is supposed to at the most basic level of functionality. It tests small, independent parts of your code for their individual expected behavior, under the assumption that when you put together a bunch of well-tested parts, they should function in an expected manner.

Generally speaking, you will run unit tests alongside the code while developing software. They should be easily runnable and be complete in a matter of minutes, whether they run locally or on a testing service. Your test runner should also allow you to mark and select which tests will run.

However, if your code doesn't sound like this, consider refactoring your code for testability, not just by your test suite but also by yourself and fellow developers. Break up your code into small logical functions that can be individually tested. We have all seen crazy-long functions with a bird's nest of logic blocks making it almost impossible to follow the method through to its natural execution. If you break the code up, it is easier not only to run the code while developing and testing locally but also to follow along in a debugger or in the human brain.

Planning how your function works under normal conditions as well as in unexpected situations achieves something vital—the unexpected is no longer unexpected. You have elevated it to expected status. Think about how you react when something expected, rather than unexpected, happens in production. It's a feeling of control over your career, destiny, and happiness. Your system must react in a predictable way for your happiness to be predictable as well.

 ### Safety Within Boundaries

Processes are better with bounds. If it is unlikely an order on your system would ever be above $100,000, it might make sense to limit such an order from being created. Why are you turning down revenue? Quite the opposite. Even though you can refund the customer, some card processing options such as Stripe do not refund processing fees, even if a transaction was done by mistake. You are trying to prevent an event that should not occur from occurring that can cost your organization money.

Another thing to test is operational bounds of the code. You may have a monolith that runs in multiple forms (e.g., client API, internal admin dashboard, task server). You can enforce boundaries such as ensuring that the admin endpoints are never accessible on the client API and vice versa. Pairing such business logic with security-minded unit tests helps harden your application and improve your security posture.

Integration testing

Before attempting to merge your code, you'll first want to run the full test suite over the code. Testing how two (or more) components or systems interact with each other with actual live network calls (or cached replays) is known as *integration testing*.

This is where you test the links between systems. In your unit tests, you assume that the libraries you are using, such as one for an API, will work as expected. You support that assumption by having integration tests that make sure that the external request actually works, possibly by making a real request to a test version for that system (or a separate testing account on a live system). Alternatively you may utilize mock versions of external systems, using a library to generate mocks by intercepting requests to a test version of a service.

There are ways in which you can run your code so that it targets managed services in the cloud and locally for offline development and testing. But you may not need to put together a true local cloud environment to test all the functionality of all of the integrations that are possible in the walled garden of your cloud provider.

How do you know that a lambda fires for every event in an integration? How do you know your cloud provider runs your code at all?

I am not suggesting you using a local cloud simulation is not helpful for avoiding issues in production. What I am suggesting is that you *may* not need it. In unit testing you are testing small, discrete units of code, and you don't want to get tied up in the details of other side effects of a highly intertangled and interdependent environment that runs a small subset of your provider's vast offerings. You can test that putting a file into a bucket triggers your code, for example, but that is not the most important part of your app. Instead, test that the side effect of one function is to put a file into a bucket, and then that when a second function is invoked as a result of this, the first does what it needs to. These functions can be tested individually, locally, and using mocks instead of a LocalStack. LocalStack would be the best choice if you did want to run your development system offline while targeting AWS.

Serverless systems that rely heavily on managed services must also rely heavily on testing the integration with those services. With payment models that let you pay only for your usage, you have no excuse not to test such dependencies and components in the cloud. Yes, you can use things like LocalStack to speed the development and testing, but either way you should let your code air out in staging first.

Mocks

Instead of talking to live systems during the execution of your test suite, you can generate *mocks*, or fake data, for staging and testing.

In the case of function invocations coming from your cloud provider, reference their docs or search around. You may be tempted to capture event payloads from real events using logging, but remember to encrypt them using the patterns suggested in Chapter 9 and sanitize them before committing them into your source control.

End-to-end testing

Testing the process from one end to the other is known appropriately as *end-to-end testing*. This is effectively one long integration test comprised of multiple steps. For an ecommerce site, you may have a test that involves some searching, shopping, adding items to the cart, and checking out. You may have this for both logged-out and logged-in users. You may have one with a longstanding cookie and one where you log in directly into the flow. These can also serve as smoke tests, which we will cover later. Such a test may also involve ensuring the end-to-end operation of your website or graphical application, so it might involve testing the user interface.

UI testing

UI testing is when you utilize tools to run and inspect the *graphical user interface* (GUI) of your application. For example, you can automate a testing suite of actions in the browser to ensure that the user interface will be correct. Sometimes, seeing a visual confirmation that a task is complete is as important to test as the task being complete. This is called *headless testing* because the test suite generally doesn't show up on a monitor. Serverless has actually become a great environment for running such headless browsers and testing suites, which used to involve keeping expensive beefy servers (browsers sure do love RAM) on standby.

Because of the separation of concerns, you should be able to test your user interface against a mock, local, or staging source of truth because a UI test can still be discrete instead of becoming an end-to-end test.

Smoke testing

Smoke testing is the method in which you test the regular functionality of a system by performing a set of normal operations and watching your monitoring dashboard for the digital equivalent of smoke—metrics informing you of an anomalous situation.

You wouldn't reassemble an engine without making sure it fires up when you're done. You'd let it run for 10 minutes, maybe drive it around, and if it doesn't smoke, then it passes the test. The same is true for your code.

Why not get started on better testing by documenting the process of one of these smoke tests? Then, see if you can build a tool that does it for you. Ready for the pro level? Have a function fire periodically to test as well. This is especially helpful when you are pre-revenue or pre-users. Should it fail open or closed? If it fails, should it warn or should it roll back?

For a proper smoke test, exercise the regular expected functionality of either a part or all of your system, live and in production. You may also smoke test your smoke tests in staging to make sure they work. The idea is, if something is broken, it should start to smoke. That allows you to observe and control this behavior before it becomes a problem.

If possible, automate the process, but check the result every time you deploy. There should be no exceptions unless you get your CI/CD to run the smoke test suite and roll back if it causes any anomalies. This type of automation can be achieved using blue/green or canary deploys, which were covered in Chapter 8.

After deploying, validate that the new version is running, and use the system by running a series of critical or popular actions. Open up your browser to make sure that your fix or feature works as expected. Does that click take an extra 100 ms? Does it look like it's starting to hang?

You don't *have* to do testing, of course. But if you don't test or don't test adequately, your users will become the testers. And if they are also the end user or the decision-maker of using your service or application, you might lose them. But, hey, that means less testing!

Testing Your Failure Strategy

If you are developing a *highly available* or *resilient* system that is supposed to be fault tolerant, make sure to test that it actually is. There are many tools for *chaos engineering*, where components of your system are terminated arbitrarily to test resilience.

Some teams forget or neglect to adequately test their failure behaviors, especially since testing them can lead to a failure. But if you don't test, you won't know. Make sure that in addition to being mindful about the sequence of events your system will take to detect and adapt to failure, those steps and sequences can and have been reproduced, preferably with automation.

But don't stop there. Make sure you plan and test the recovery sequences, as well as for an extended outage. Organizations with multiregion services may run exercises that actually shut off access from employees and an entire region of their cloud provider, as well as cut off access between regions for the servers. When in doubt, test it out!

Code Coverage

While some managers and organizations swear by the *code coverage* metric, it's not fully useful in itself. "Coverage" simply indicates the percentage of application code that is executed during a run of a test suite, usually just the unit test suite, which is not part of the test suite itself. Don't get me wrong: this is an incredibly important metric, but without the enforcement of the quality of those tests through a strict process of code (or peer) review, they may actually decrease the overall quality. In a project with an *object-relational mapping* (ORM) system, such as Django, simply running an empty test suite may give the impression that a lot of the model code is already covered. This means it runs but is not really tested. It will likely prevent against syntax and basic execution errors, but it has given no indication that the code does what it is supposed to do. It just tells you that you have a valid model syntax.

Set a standard for your projects to have for code coverage to get started, even if it is 50% and a simple rule that all new code and changes must have accompanying test coverage (if you are not doing this already). Then bump up that number as you see fit. Many teams settle around a goal of 90% and that all new pull or merge requests have fully covered code. Even when patching production with a hotfix, the procedure should be to write a test that reproduces the error occurring in production and commit it to your branch with the test failing. Make a commit with the fix, and that test should succeed. Then after peer review, you can responsibly and frantically push it, hoping that it fixes everything. But really, that only works if the rest of the code is well covered by tests, and you validate the fix in staging.

Configuration itself should sometimes be considered as code when calculating coverage. You should include different expected values for settings variables, such as a value for a promotional offer setting. Different expected values or ranges should be tested for functionality. A configuration that is truly just that does not need to be tested.

Changing how to connect to the database is important, and an invalid configuration should be prevented from deployment. But that is not what needs to be tested. Some configuration is really not that at all. Have a YAML or JSON file that changes the execution of code in production? It's generally static, like a source code file, and does not get changed or configured per the environment. Its functionality may be covered by other tests, but that file being walked and executed during the test suite is important and should be measured, if possible.

Test-Driven Development (TDD)

Which came first, the method or its test? I like to write out a skeleton of the code first. I might even keep writing out my skeleton until it has achieved some level of progress, and then I solidify that progress by writing the tests immediately after. There is no perfect workflow for integrating tests, but at least give TDD a try.

You can run a specific test module, group of tests, or a single test using the command line. The package `pytest-fastest` provides this exact functionality. Combined with the `--pdb` flag, you'll have a streamlined workflow.

Power Up Your Testing

Nobody likes a slow testing suite. It becomes a burden and needs to be maintained just as any other part of your system. Make sure to empower your test suite with configurations or plug-ins that help you parallelize tests to run faster. By utilizing multiple processes, your tests will run in a fraction of the time.

But, over time, as they slow down, you can use plug-ins to ensure that your tools report the speed of tests alongside the top slowest tests (as an encouragement for others to help improve these tests). Other plug-ins can format the output for easier consumption, such as outputting JUnit for Jenkins, so that your test runner can specifically mention which tests fail and that can show up in the code review. You might need to set up your test database or test database bootstrapping process to allow for multiple test cases to make sure that even though tests are run concurrently, each process running tests in a serial manner (one at a time) won't affect the tests or test data of the other processes.

Staging

The real purpose of the scientific method is to make sure nature hasn't misled you into thinking you know something you actually don't know.

    —Robert M. Pirsig, *Zen and the Art of Motorcycle Maintenance: An Inquiry into Values* (HarperTorch)

How do you know that a piece of code you intend to run in production operated the same way it did when you ran it locally? Shipping code to production can be a leap of faith. Sure, the age of containers has brought the ability to package software so that it can run the same in all places, but that doesn't help with the constellation of real-world dependencies on systems whose state is always changing.

A presentation by an Apple engineer at its Worldwide Developers Conference (WWDC) last year discussed the exponential nature of state growth as a factorial of all events possible. The presentation discussed the design of the Swift UI, a declarative model for creating views in Swift applications similar to Facebook's React for browser-based applications. The engineer gave an example of a simple detail view in an iOS application that allows for four events, or actions, to occur, and then demonstrated the complications of predicting the combinations of events to achieve a given state and the difficulty in UI bugs that don't crash. Perhaps you've written amazingly idempotent actions and stateless services, but your production environment does, in fact, have a state, no matter how much you attempt to factor it out. So you need a production-like environment where you can stage your code.

Staging is an environment where you can stage your code to validate its preparedness for going into production, thereby increasing your confidence in your code even further. Simplifying the factors you have to consider when something isn't working in production is the ultimate goal of parity between staging and production. The purpose is not only to stage that code and see if it stands up before going to production but also to prevent incidents and outages and shorten the time to resolution of any such incidents.

The cost of maintaining a high-fidelity staging environment is one of the most common business cases against it. That concern fades in the cloud, thanks to on-demand resources. Serverless should end that case entirely. If your company cannot justify the cost of a proper staging environment given serverless tools, it may not be able to justify your salary, as it will be spent dealing with preventable issues in production.

There is simply no excuse to not have some reliable form of staging. It does not need to have perfect production parity, and it may not have the same volumes of types of data (see the privacy section in Chapter 9), but how else could you test your deploy process without a staging environment that at least mirrors production? You could use canary or blue/green patterns, but how would you even test that your canary system works without testing it in staging first? If you don't know your canary rollback doesn't work until you really need it, you're going to have big troubles.

In real estate, many sellers or agents will stage a house with furniture. It gives you a better idea of how your routines and preferences will work out in a new environment. Not only does it help reduce the cognitive load of buyers imagining their new living arrangements, but it makes it easier to envision themselves performing common household activities. That is exactly what staging can do for the confidence of your software.

Not only is it the best place to first test your production code other than actual production, but it also forces engineers to think about it as the target environment instead of the default target environment of their favorite localhost. There is no home like 127.0.0.1 after all, but one day your code will have to leave the nest and survive on its own without the helicopter parenting support that you provide locally.

Correctly configuring your code and avoiding arbitrary hardcoded values becomes really important as you plan to run your software in multiple environments. The same preparation you undertake to prepare your code for local development, testing, and production is how you prepare your app for staging. (This book doesn't cover the advanced concepts involved in getting your application fully *production ready*. For that, I recommend Susan Fowler's *Production-Ready Microservices*.)

So how do you set up your staging environment? If you've been following along with the best practices in the book so far, it should all be very easy, with one large exception—data. Not only is data the hardest part, it can also be contentious or regulated. I will get into further detail once we cover the easy stuff.

Why is having a staging environment easy? Your infrastructure and deployment code should be automated to the point that all you have to do is add a new stage and possibly tweak some of the configuration settings related to that stage. The settings to tweak are usually a trade-off between achieving full production and staging parity (a difficult feat considering staging may lack any real user traffic or pressure) and keeping that pesky cloud bill in check. With serverless functions, you do not have to worry about running costly infrastructure at idle all of the time. But if you depend on *instance-backed* services, where you specify and pay for a specific type of server, you may choose to lower instance types. Keep in mind, however, that this goes against achieving the fidelity that is the basis of our staging swagger. How will you know how your code performs when it doesn't have the same CPU or RAM? You might not need to. You can use blue/green or canary deployment strategies described in Chapter 8 to avoid a degradation in performance if it is critical for your app. But it also may be the lowest priority, as the Zen of Python reminds us to avoid premature optimization. Consider what's acceptable for your use case and your budget.

You will need to make difficult choices when dealing with other services and data, the most difficult of which is: should staging use our production secrets and production data? Take the payment processor Stripe. It offers a distinct test environment for all of its users that allows testing credit cards and rejects real ones. This is the exact opposite behavior of its main or production environment. If you want to test payments in your staging environment, do you want to use real cards or fake ones? Even when the choice is clear, this type of decision must be made for every behavior in your system where the development version and production version differ.

Even your database choice may not be straightforward. You may choose to point your staging settings at the real production database. If you are in an organization that espouses the practice of only rolling forward, never backward, and want to run a cutting-edge beta with limited access that is part of the real production environment, is that really staging?

Staging is whatever your organization wants and needs it to be. There is really no definitive answer. The consensus is for more similarity or fidelity to production, while being fully isolated from production.

Why isolation? As discussed in Chapter 9, you always need to limit your blast radius. Make sure that the code in your staging environment is not relying on or accessing the counterpart of a service that lives in your staging environment. And if you are using sensitive user data in your staging environment, access needs to be controlled in a similar fashion to data in production.

Which brings us to the hard part: should your staging environment use real, synthetic, or sanitized user data?

If engineers can't access user data in production but can access a full copy of it in a less-restrictive environment (staging), those controls in production are not protecting the data. Keep in mind that if your production environment has controls limiting access to sensitive data, your staging should as well, for fidelity and the ability to test new versions or revisions of those controls themselves before they cause an incident in production.

A year from reading this book, you may have a great application or service and need to make a change to its infrastructure or configuration, possibly by changing its *serverless.yml* file. You want to add the latest, shiniest tech because it's missing from your CV, and thankfully the community has put in the hard work for a great plug-in that makes it a breeze. The only problem? The plug-in is too new for the version of the deployment tool, in this case the serverless framework, to work. Should you update it and immediately try to deploy to production?

The answer is likely yes, because you should be keeping your dependencies up to date for security purposes and because you can't let this change be tested for the first time in production. Unless you spend way too much time writing tests instead of shipping features, your testing suites will not cover such a change. They may be able to fail invalid syntax in your *serverless.yml* (a great idea), and your deployment pipeline should catch the deployment failure, but by then it's too late. You have potentially introduced an inconsistent state in the cloud that you have to manually resolve before you can even attempt another deployment.

Take the time to think about the repercussions and trade-offs of your staging design and practices. If the staging database is constantly wiped and replaced with a sanitized copy of production, you may miss out on bugs that only exist once testing actions have had the chance to age.

Conclusion

Art is anything you can do well. Anything you can do with quality.
　　—Robert M. Pirsig, *Zen and the Art of Motorcycle Maintenance: An Inquiry into Values* (HarperTorch)

Never forget the return achieved by how much time you invest into your tools. Testing is just another tool in your virtual workshop. So is staging. Feel free to find the right level of testing, but I can guarantee you that level is never zero hours.

The more confidence you have in your code, the less time you will spend debugging and wishing you could easily SSH into your distributed system.

CHAPTER 11

Planning for Failure

Enterprise software must be cynical. Cynical software expects bad things to happen and is never surprised when they do. Cynical software doesn't even trust itself, so it puts up internal barriers to protect itself from failures. It refuses to get too intimate with other systems, because it could get hurt.

—Michael T. Nygard, *Release It!*, 2nd Edition (Pragmatic Bookshelf)

Plan for failure. This chapter will provide you the basics of planning for operational failures, and the rest of the book will help you avoid and detect such anomalies, but remember this: *failures are not anomalies.* An anomaly is an occurrence that deviates from standard behavior, but you can reduce failures by planning for them as standard operating behavior. This is how you build a system that outlives the time you spend building it.

Introduction: Understand It, Even if You Don't Manage It

It is not your responsibility to run these managed services, but you need to understand how they work. Just because you can copy and paste some code into the dashboard of your cloud provider, doesn't mean you don't need to think about Unix file permissions. Upload a deployment package to AWS Lambda that is not world readable, and it won't run. Compile a dependency on your macOS machine and get a nice surprising error when it doesn't run on the serverless platform. "But I don't compile dependencies for my dynamically run language!" Try to manipulate an image, use cryptography, or connect to an RDBMS database, and you might discover that your successful deployment wasn't quite so successful.

It doesn't matter if this affects you or not; it is important as the designer to understand the environment and system running your code in the same way you have to understand the language you are using, the libraries you are using, and how the customers are going to access your system as well.

The system takes on a life of its own and can continue to grow due to this thoughtful planning, including the most thoughtful aspect of planning: making the ideas and information necessary for the system to operate available in documentation. If it doesn't have a runbook, is it really production ready? A real production system needs a runbook, which is an operator's manual for the system itself. I will explain this concept further in this chapter, as well as cover failure points in more depth.

What happens to your system if you get hit by a bus? People might expect it to keep running. This dark commonality in software engineering is not just limited to software. How did Coca-Cola keep running after the original inventor passed? Someone wrote down the recipe. The recipe is so valuable, it is locked in a vault that is only accessible by a few people.

Software is mutable. It changes, adapts, evolves, and lives. Even if yours doesn't, all of the other software it relies on does change, so you need to plan for that. If you are reading this book, you hopefully agree that the best software design for your use case might be software that is changeable. That is why people usually accept the trade-off of functions or microservices: because mutability and the speed of development are the priority. As you write software at this increased pace, don't forget about what happens when people who didn't build it have to go back and understand it, change it, or both. You're building a business: it can't be one that only works if you use it on Greg's MacBook after he chants a set of secret incantations. If you want your business to last, you want your software to last.

You still can move fast! Set an expectation for the system(s) you are building. My first large serverless system was designed to handle 10 million users, and a certain number of concurrent new user registrations. "What happens after that?" many asked me. I responded: "I am building for a specific goal. I will need to make trade-offs to achieve that goal given the constraints." In the same spirit of being constrained to a ship date, we are constrained to a certain level of performance. We are not irresponsible. We will monitor the number of users (and other metrics) to determine when, how, and what it will take to get to the next order of magnitude. If you are building a startup from scratch, and have the luxury, design for a million users. Total users? Monthly actives? That is up to you and your teams. But don't design for one user: Greg.

Identify Risks

How important is your system? Will someone die if it goes down or behaves unpredictably? That is the the most important question for anyone involved in the design or business of your system. Your customers can help you gain additional insight.

You need to know what happens when your system goes down. This could range from a failure queue backing up, to the disruption of the entire global economy. How likely is your system to go down? You can take this under consideration when designing your system, and you can also test your system to provide further insight, but due to the entropy of nature, this will always be an educated guess. So let's get educated.

What might cause this system to go down? There are entire books dedicated to this topic. The epitaph from the beginning of the chapter is from my favorite, *Release It!*. The next chapter will provide further depth, but for the purpose of this chapter, your system is merely a collection of failure points that can and will fail in different ways, at different times, and with different severities. Since every situation is different, the following is an exercise to help you discover the answer to these important questions.

Exercise: Finding Your Failure Points

Here is an exercise to get you started. Make a list of all of the things that could break in your system. If you don't have a system you are currently working on, either use an existing project or think of what you want to build with serverless. Next to that, write a score of 1-10 of how likely it would be to happen. Then write down what would happen if it broke. Table 11-1 shows an example list. We can't always control everything in the left column, or the middle column, or even the right column. But asking yourself this question might change how you approach system design. Sometimes, improving your system design isn't about cracking open *Cracking the Coding Interview* by Gayle Laakmann McDowell (CareerCup), but simplifying the system as much as possible. If you understand the trade-offs in every decision, and document those trade-offs and why they seemed like the right decision at the time, you will likely save yourself massive effort over time. This is how you get to sleep through the night without a 2 A.M. call.

Table 11-1. Example table for this exercise

Ways your system can break	Likelihood	Impact
Large and persistent traffic spike from a marketing or PR campaign	8	Lost customers, wasted effort
Database gets corrupted	5	Lost data, lost revenue, lost time
Database gets corrupted and backups don't restore correctly	3	Find a new job
Certain long-running tasks don't complete and block other tasks	7	Weird side effects that cause you to wake up at 2 A.M.

Take a moment to reflect on what you have come up with. What did you learn about the fragility of your system? Is your system resilient, or would it break for someone with the last name "Null"?[1] Investing time in sussing out your failure points is

---

1 B. Barrett, "How a *NULL* License Plate Landed One Hacker in Ticket Hell," *Wired*, August 13, 2019, *https://oreil.ly/B-aS3*.

imperative in building a resilient system. If you found this exercise difficult, try it out as a brainstorming session with members of your team. Next we will discuss how to best identify risks.

Be Prepared

Banks have been described as "too big to fail," but they really do back that up with documentation. To illustrate this point, let's pull up an interesting document known as a "Resolution Plan" that is filed regularly with the federal government and is almost a runbook in itself. But it's actually a living will (*https://oreil.ly/pBDsa*):

> Each plan, commonly known as a living will, must describe the company's strategy for rapid and orderly resolution in the event of material financial distress or failure of the company, and include both public and confidential sections.

Figure 11-1 is from JPMorgan Chase's 2017 public resolution plan. It is 170 pages long, and this is just the public version. So if we read this document, what do we find? More runbooks!

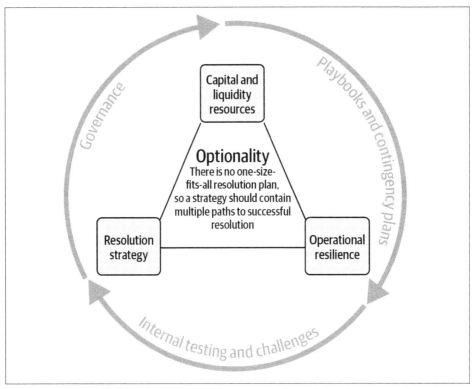

Figure 11-1. Chase's Crisis Management Framework from their 2017 Resolution Plan Public Filing, featuring "playbooks"

Making a Runbook

Write on-call runbooks that sleepy developers can understand at 2 A.M.
  —Susan J. Fowler, *Production-Ready Microservices* (O'Reilly)

What is it that people hate about 2 A.M.? Oh yeah, working at 2 A.M. We should try and avoid that. My personal philosophy is that I write software so that no one will wake me up in the middle of the night. But when it happens, a runbook is the best way to get back to sleep as quickly as possible.

A *runbook*, or an operator's manual, is a document created by the developers of a system to give instructions to the operators of a system. Even if those are the same people. It should be a living document that continues to be maintained and expanded by both parties. The developers must be the owners and initial creators of the document, and the operators should contribute and artifact knowledge gained from operating the system. The developers can use this information to improve the operation of the system.

At the very minimum, a runbook should provide the following:

Overview
  What did we build and why?

Service contract
  What is the expected behavior for this system? How are other systems supposed to interact with it? What guarantees are made about the durability, reliability, or availability of this service? Even if that means no guarantees.

Software functionality
  How does the software work, and how are contributors expected to develop the software further? Useful information about local testing and development.

Operational functionality
  How does this software work in Production and Staging? What infrastructure does it rely on? How does it get deployed? How is it expected to run?

Monitoring/observability
  What information can you see about the state of the system and its performance? Where can you find these metrics and what do they mean? What are the alerting expectations? What does it mean if something is running out of bounds? What is the process for updating these expected values and alarms?

How to tell when something isn't working
  Clear indications of failure states based on the data available in the previous section.

What to do when something isn't working

What are the common actions an operator might take to resolve an issue? What actions do you want the operator to first take to better understand and remediate the situation? If you can get the operator to resolve the issue with just the runbook, you get to stay asleep. Also, consider what actions could be automated to have the system self-heal (as well as what indicators an operator needs to know to intervene manually).

Operations you can perform on the system

What steps can an operator take to investigate behavior, fix an issue, or bring back the system from a complete failure? These should have some form of organization, but most importantly should have an identifier for each operation so you can reference them elsewhere in the runbook. For example, when alarm X goes above Y, run process Z to see if it resolves itself within N minutes (specificity is important when it is important, and not important any other time).

Undocumented knowledge

What do you need to know that isn't in the vendor docs? Why are we using that obscure setting? Why did we turn off the default feature in X? What obscure Stack Overflow incantation did process X take to get working? When and why did that become a problem?

Team/project/company-specific knowledge

What promises did we make to Legal or Security when designing the system? What trade-offs did we make and why? When should those be revisited? We purposely did not store X for concerns from Team Y. They said we could revisit that decision in Q4 2020 based on Z.

Does this seem like a lot of work as you try and rush something out the door? Here is an idea: start the document when you start designing the service, fill it in as you go along, and then you won't have to rush anything out the door.

Planning for Outages

No matter how much work gets put into planning for failure, if your system reaches some level of success it will eventually have some form of outage. Being able to easily track down the right point of contact is critical to successfully handling an incident. In addition to the runbook, a production system should have a plan for reaching a human when such intervention is required.

On-Call/Escalation Plan

This plan can be as simple or complicated as it needs to be for the use case, but a good plan must have some form of redundancy or escalation. Only having one contact, while being a serious deficiency for mission-critical applications, may be the only option you have available on a small team. In a larger organization, however, it is a common practice to have your alarm *fail up* the org chart until someone acknowledges it. The first thing that person may do (other than checking the runbook) is try and get hold of the others the alarm failed to reach.

But wait. We are software engineers. We should try and automate as much of this as possible. (We cover this further in Chapter 6.) There are tools that will take your alarms and execute the on-call plan you have determined. In fact, they will even help you get started with some of the most common ones available.

There are rare conditions where your cloud provider might need to reach out to you. In these situations, failure to respond can lead to data loss or even more catastrophic situations. Make sure your contact information is up to date. Use distribution lists (and make sure external domains can reach them as well), and give them an email that opens a PagerDuty incident. Even if you don't have a service contract, they may need to reach out to your for legal reasons, such as a violation of their terms of service. If you do not remediate or respond in time, they can suspend or close your account (it might make sense to have multicloud backups). Add a quarterly action item to your operational procedures to test these contact methods and to make sure all of the information on these accounts is up to date. Get creative with the ways you test all parts of the stack, and maybe ask them to try to reach you by opening a service ticket. I have "heard" all sorts of stories from a "friend": an external website claims abuse coming from your system, the cloud provider approved a service limit but didn't have the capacity in a certain region to support it, and anything else you can imagine. It may not be your job to handle this, but it is your job to ship the most reliable system in your control. Don't let something simple like this destroy your system, its data, your company's reputation, or your company.

Monitor Your Cloud Provider

Shared responsibility is the most important thing to understand when relying on other people to run your servers, but it is widely misunderstood. The basic concept is that you are responsible for what is *in* the cloud, and your provider is responsible for the security *of* the cloud. The cloud itself is not magic. It is regular hardware and software managed by regular people. Given a long enough timeline, your system will run into every possible problem imaginable. Your cloud provider can suffer an outage, but a minor service degradation could be more damaging to your application if you have not designed for its failure, and don't have any monitoring to discover these issues before they turn into larger incidents.

Know Your (Service) Limits

Knowing the limits of the services you are planning to rely on for your own reliability and resilience are paramount to success. Before you choose a package, library, language, or even a keyboard, do the research to make sure it's going to work (or at least that you can return it if it doesn't). Before you integrate with another service or API inside your own company, or from even someone with the stature of Stripe or Twilio, you have to make sure it will do what you are expecting it to do.

Let's walk through an example of what happens if you ignore this advice. Imagine utilizing a queue from your cloud vendor that has an option for visibility time-outs. You implement a proper exponential backoff to the delight of everyone around you. When a service you rely on starts throwing around 502 errors, you investigate and decide to ignore the alert. Everything resolves itself. What a well-designed system.

This keeps happening for the next year until things start to go crazy. Do you know how many messages your queue allows you to have in flight (invisible) at any given time? Did you know your queue even had a limit for such a thing?

You are used to unidirectionally communicating limits all the time to your colleagues and customers. Well, you are the customer in this situation. So read the service limits before you solidify any immutable choices that you make.

You may want to take this advice one step further. If you want to learn how to build a scalable system, look no further than the artifacts published by your cloud provider. The service limits tell you the trade-offs they had to make in designing the service. They can't defy the laws of physics or computing with their services, and neither can you. The pages of their documentation are full of lessons no matter where you are in your software career.

Conclusion

Planning for failure is a critical part of the success of your system, as it takes on a life of its own in production. But all of that work may be for naught if it is not documented and readily accessible to a human who is paged to intervene in your system. They may not know that it's OK for your normally dormant function to burst to a concurrency of 1,000 and get throttled after some other big event. And that this behavior, while a cause for alarm in some settings, is designed to self-heal. We covered the topic of how to design your alarms in Chapter 6, but it is a topic of much nuance and no correct answers, and it will take time for you to find what works best for your team or project.

CHAPTER 12

Conclusion

Everything has an end, except sausage, which has two.
—Dada Land, September 2019

Our journey together is coming to an end. To close out the book, let's look at a framework for making decisions about vendors and technologies in general. Then I will walk you through how you might apply certain key concepts from this book differently based on which hosted or self-hosted options you use.

Remember that, as with all marketing speak, the promises of serverless don't apply universally. Be on the lookout for such language as a sign that people are hyping a technology about which they only have a shallow understanding. Instead, try to translate it into what it really means. For example, "you only pay for what you use" is really "you don't have to pay for idle capacity." But of course that cost does get factored into the pricing offered by your cloud provider: even marketing speak has to obey the laws of physics. Idle capacity has to be powered, provisioned, and accounted for in a multitude of ways. So it really comes down to throwing money at the problem.

Managing a data center is complicated, no matter how much experience your organization may have with it. Doing so may not provide any additional lift or value to the internal or end users of your system, so if there is a reliable way to abstract the problem away, that may be in your best interest. The same goes for servers. Sure, it's best to pick purpose-fit solutions when possible. So serverless may not be the best use case. But anyone who believes in the public cloud and its merits should do the same for serverless.

There's a common metaphor in the tech industry that refers to managing a fleet of servers in terms of animals: we've gone from treating servers like pets to treating them like cattle. Well, I am here to say that now is a great time to go vegan. (Or at least to be more vegan more of the time.)

If you have ever tried using a virtual reality headset for a long enough time, you have likely found yourself adjusting to your new reality. Once your mind becomes enveloped inside a new environment, it rewires and adapts. Serverless is the new reality. It's here. It's not just a trend. It's also the spiritual return of CGI-BIN: now that the fundamental issue with CGI-BIN has been repaired by the return of a distributed executable, in this case the container, the history becomes the future.

Deciding among Vendors

To some, the cloud is the natural evolution of servers being available for rent by the hour, minute, or even second. This evolution brought us to serverless and to compute time billed in milliseconds. But those who just view the cloud this way are not using it to its full potential. Think about why you are choosing the cloud or serverless in the first place. Make sure those reasons are first and foremost in your considerations; they likely should carry the most weight in your final decision.

You are not just choosing between all of the providers, but between all of their offerings (or groups of offerings). You might start to build your application in one of the clouds, but decide some background work or data processing can be best done elsewhere—which may also provide enhanced disaster recovery as well.

Remember that your team, like the teams building search at the App Store or at Google, have different requirements and resources. Remember that using serverless is a choice like any other choice, complete with trade-offs.

Part of being a professional is about on-demand performance. A major league baseball player gets paid the big bucks because they can produce the hits. Same with experienced engineers. That's the bar you should set for any services, libraries, technologies, and frameworks you choose in the time of your development. Remember that the bar for your dependencies needs to be at least as high, if not higher, than your project's bar.

Don't just think about the current offering of a vendor; consider the rate of change of that offering and how it will improve or stagnate over time. You also need to do the same for your own requirements, as they too will change as a function of time.

A smaller, more ambitious provider might see you as representing their target customer as they try to find product/market fit; they might be willing to build custom options for you that others would charge an arm and a leg for, or tell you that what you want is coming, but in some mythical quarter that will be delayed indefinitely. However, you might not need that kind of customization or attention. If you just want reliability, you may need the market leader.

Does the provider offer robust tooling? Do you want to be locked into it anyway or do you want another choice that can support the shift to multiple clouds? What about the infrastructure and templating tools?

How easy is it to set up the kind of reliability and availability that first made you choose the public cloud? How do replication and recovery work? How easy is the tooling around it all? How hard is it to manage the virtual networking aspects of your cloud services?

Turn to the "deep dive" presentations from the cloud providers to better understand the systems and services you'll be relying on, as well as to learn more about interesting architectures designed to achieve a certain objective at scale. (DynamoDB's system of tokens for writes is interesting, for example.)

Community

An important element in any technology decision is the community. Any technology's community provides knowledge, advancement, and will be the source of extra tooling or your future teammates.

The community helps ensure that you have tools to make your life easier. The tools your provider offers will generally not be as wonderful as you would expect, although there are some exceptions to that rule. Factor in all available supported tools when comparing how you will manage your cloud, because you have to manage even your managed services.

Gather the Advice of Others

Ask other smart people around you. Ask colleagues and former colleagues. Seek out people in communities like Hacker News. Ask a college professor. Ask a job interviewer when they ask you for questions.

You should always be learning. Help others to always be learning too. Keep reading, teaching, and mentoring. Try to get your employer to pay for books or subscriptions (both technical and nontechnical) that will directly increase the value you provide to the organization. Leave books on your desk, share them, read them in public spaces at the office. Let people know by your actions that you are actively seeking to improve yourself. If your employer paid for the book, give it away to a coworker when you are done, with the condition they should do the same. Acquire and read books that are outside the scope of value to your current role as well, and maintain a personal list or library of books to recommend that improve personal or professional skills as well as technical ones.

Get good at bad code. The essayist Paul Graham suggests (*https://oreil.ly/VVwtv*) that any writer looking to improve their craft should "become a connoisseur of bad writing." The more you appreciate bad code and why it is bad, the more you can understand and identify its problems and attempt to turn it into "good" code. Good code and good writing are both easily understood and achieve an objective in the minimum amount of argument (or lines, if you will). Search for people who are having problems with the technologies you're interested in, to balance out all of the excited marketing hype.

Try to find things that you do repetitively, and automate them if it makes sense. While it's funny, the *xkcd* comic "Is It Worth the Time?" could almost become an ISO standard (see Figure 8-1). Realize that you are part of the pipeline of your project and are worthy of the investment. That scales, too, because you can share that automation with others. Even doing something like speeding up your test suite can almost best be debated by referencing this table. Remember, too, that you must know what you are doing manually first, and have confidence at it, in order to automate.

There is no such thing as a simple change. Even with the confidence gained through thoughtful design, automation, testing, and staging, there is still a chance things will not work.

What to Do When You Get Stuck

Take a break from the situation, if possible. You need to spend time enjoying programming if you don't feel that way at work. Learn new things, or just build or tinker for fun. Try to make some things that make your life better. Share them online. Welcome the community.

Ask the community for help. Learn. Share knowledge. Repeat.

Search for others facing the same issue by looking at the issues for that repository. Make sure to check both open and closed issues. Consider creating a new one. Make sure not to leak any sensitive data in doing so, and to follow any policies of your organization.

Be grateful to those who share the work, sometimes with no compensation other than the satisfaction of helping others or bettering themselves.

Taking the Next Step in Your Career

Take charge of your career, but don't let it change who you are. Favor personal growth and mutual respect over winning the shallow favor and approval of those around you. Be the coworker people want to work with, and your career will be limitless. As your experience and your craft increase over time, you can play the politics game and get promoted, but do it with honor. Find and help others in your organization in ways that aren't directly related to your current position or title. The best way to be promoted is to perform at that level and take on those responsibilities. Those around you should support you as you get promoted; if not, maybe you want to find a new job. Life is too short for pettiness, and quality software engineers are scarce.

Find work that pays you fairly for what you know, but that allows and even expects you to learn and grow. Repeat. Don't be afraid of not knowing all the answers—that's an impossibility in this field. Share and be inclusive in your decision making. Let others help guide the decision, since they will likely have to live with its repercussions. Don't be selfish.

Decide if you are in it for a sprint or a marathon—not in terms of a single job, but your career as a whole. Some people really just want to make as much money as possible so they'll never have to work again, and they tend to leave collateral damage (externalities) in their wake.

When conducting interviews, be open to the possibility of learning something or being wrong. You want to hire people who are better than you in at least some way that you can learn from, even if you wind up competing with them for promotions later. And you should return the favor to those teammates. Everyone on the team will benefit from keeping the bar high.

Sometimes you will have to spend time at work learning new things and not producing any immediately measurable results. Account for this time as you would any other type of work.

Write down your thoughts. Keep a log of actions you take when solving a new problem, especially when putting out a fire in production. It will help with your pacing and your decision making, and it'll certainly help you produce and share an accurate and detailed postmortem.

Finally, remember that the production system that you ship or work on is a living, breathing thing.

Index

A

access limitations, 139-140
access logs, 103, 111
ADRs (see architectural decision records (ADRs))
alerting, 36, 87, 95-96
Amazon
  cloud services offerings, 24
  shared responsibility model, 135
Amazon API Gateway, 56
Amazon Resource Name (ARN), 69
Amazon Web Services (AWS), 25
  Amazon Resource Name (ARN), 69
  AWS Layers, 147
  CloudFormation
    template deployment, 120
    weaknesses of, 66
  Lambda, 23
    cold starts, 29
    compute time limitations, 29
    DeadLetterErrors pane, 98-99
  as leading provider, 66
  reputation as cloud services provider, 24
  Simple Storage Service (S3), 22
  Well-Architected Framework, 30
Amazon.com, 14
anomalies, 169
API gateway, 34
App Engine, 23
application level (custom) metrics, 36, 91-92
application logs, 103
application performance monitoring (APM), 89
application programming interfaces (APIs), 58

application size limitations of serverless computing, 30
architects
  decision making, 27-30
    documentation of decisions, 28-29
    process of, 29
    timing of decisions, 30
    types of decisions, 28
  decision-making
    documentation of decisions, 30
  knowledge of, 27
  role of, 26-27
architectural decision records (ADRs), 30
architectural reviews, 30
architecture
  cloud provider components, 31-37
    API gateway, 34
    buckets, 32-33
    compute, 33
    datastores, 33
    GraphQL, 35
    identity services, 34
    logging, 36
    monitoring/alerting, 36
    networking, 35
    queues, 31-32
    state machines, 35-36
    streams, 31
  cloud provider events, 37
  explained, 25-26
  interfaces (see interfaces)
  patterns, 38-44
    background task, 41
    fanning out, 43

webhooks, 57-58
serverless, 47-48
invocations, 81
concurrency, 48
failure of, 47
types of, 47

J

K

L

M

About the Author

Jason Katzer is the creator of CloudPro.app, which creates developer productivity tools for the cloud and offers consulting on cloud native architectures and cloud cost savings. Previously, he served as director of software engineering at Capital One (Paribus/WikiBuy) and Blink Health. Jason is also a serial entrepreneur and angel investor who's been involved with and started many new ventures. He's worked for several industries, including health care, consumer tech, fitness, sales, finance, and telecom, and loves to help people save both time and money. But his one real focus is building quality software. He is a passionate teacher (MakeSchool) as well as a lifelong learner. He devours TV shows, podcasts, and audio books, and will dearly miss the voice of Vin Scully.

Colophon

The animal on the cover of *Learning Serverless* is the black-tailed godwit (*Limosa limosa*). These wide-ranging shorebirds breed in northern wetlands from Iceland in the west across Europe to Siberia in the east. A small population stays resident in northwestern Europe. Migrating birds fly south to winter across central Africa and parts of northern India, southeasternmost Asia, and coastal Australia.

Godwits are large, long-legged sandpipers, standing on average 16 inches tall, covered with black and white speckled patterning. In summer breeding plumage, their main body color is pale red; in winter they are pale gray brown. They are best distinguished while flying by their white wing bars and back. These birds forage with their long bills for small prey such as insects, worms, crustaceans, and tadpoles.

Like some other species of godwits, black-tailed godwits undertake long migration journeys between breeding and winter territories, sometimes flying at altitudes of three miles or higher, where the air contains far less oxygen than at sea level. They have been known to undertake parts of their migration flights at these high altitudes to take advantage of favorable high-level winds, among other factors. Studies have also shown that black-tailed godwits show variation as to their migratory pathways as a group as well as individually over a period of years.

The black-tailed godwit is considered Near Threatened at the global level, with many wetlands across its range being developed for agricultural use. Many of the animals on O'Reilly covers are endangered; *all of them* are important to the world.

The color illustration is by Karen Montgomery, based on a black-and-white engraving from George Shaw's *General Zoology* (1809-1826). The cover fonts are Gilroy and Guardian Sans. The text font is Adobe Minion Pro; the heading font is Adobe Myriad Condensed; and the code font is Dalton Maag's Ubuntu Mono.

O'REILLY®

There's much more where this came from.

Experience books, videos, live online training courses, and more from O'Reilly and our 200+ partners—all in one place.

Learn more at oreilly.com/online-learning

Lightning Source UK Ltd.
Milton Keynes UK
UKHW030915120821
388724UK00004B/18